Rotonda

The Vision and the Reality

A short history of a Florida development

Rotonda

The Vision and the Reality

A short history of a Florida development

Jack Alexander

Tabby House

Manufactured in the United States of America

Library of Congress Card Catalog Number: 94-38037

ISBN: 1-881539-07-5

Cover design: Pearl and Associates
The Superstars™ and Formica™ are registered trademarks.

Rotonda was produced by the
Rotonda West Property Owners Association,
supported by the Rotonda West Association
Rotonda West, Florida

Library of Congress Cataloging-in-Publication Data

Alexander, Jack, 1926-
      Rotonda : the vision and the reality : a short history of a
Florida development / Jack Alexander.
          p.   cm.
      Includes bibliographical references.
      ISBN 1-881539-07-5 : $14.95
      1. Real estate development--Florida--Charlotte County--History.
2. Rotonda West (Fla.)--History. I. Title
HD266.F62C483   1995
333.77' 15' 0975949--dc20   94-38037
                                                                    CIP

Tabby House
4429 Shady Lane
Charlotte Harbor, Florida, 33980

Contents

Preface

ON SEPTEMBER 1969, Cavanagh Leasing Corporation of Miami launched Rotonda West on Florida's Gulf Coast between Sarasota and Fort Myers, in Charlotte County. They promoted it as "one of the most exciting concepts in land planning ever devised . . . a self-contained circular community of 50,000."

A fact ignored by buyers of lots and homes at the birth of Rotonda West was the death, a few years earlier, of Rotonda East. That vision, in the Palm Beach area, fell victim to skeptical Palm Beach and Martin County authorities. It never came to fruition for reasons that should have been disturbing.

In retrospect, Rotonda East was stillborn—a victim of mismanagement, questionable sales tactics and economic and social realities. And the same management almost killed Rotonda West in its early stages, selling lots at a ratio to homes of twenty to one, far outpacing the development of supportive infrastructure and promised amenities.

Cavanagh was set back by events an alert management might have anticipated—an oil crisis that inhibited travel, a recession that spiraled interest rates upwards and restricted the money supply, federal tax code changes that stifled Florida's condominium market, and the onset of environmentalism, with new agencies and regulations targeting, particularly, developers of sensitive land. A recipe for trouble in paradise.

The early years in Rotonda West were exciting for the new residents, by most accounts. They grumbled about things that affected them directly—construction of their homes, mainly, and the chaos it caused—but they largely ignored the problems swirling around Cavanagh. They reached out and supported each other in their splendid new isolation.

They planted community roots and started their own social and church organizations.

When it became obvious that *The Vision* had been overstated, they formed their own property owners association and confronted Cavanagh at every turn.

As the early euphoria wore off, Cavanagh faced mortgage foreclosure, sought Chapter 11 bankruptcy protection, came under FTC investigation, and had to fight an increasing wave of litigation.

Today, twenty-five years old, Rotonda is a thriving community. Though less grandiose than originally conceived, it is a "happy, comfortable, neat place to live." Just ask the residents. Ask the golfers. Even the consistent complainers—the bane of any community—admit they'd rather live here than elsewhere.

To a degree, Rotonda is unique. As one developer put it, from a land assemblage point of view, "It couldn't happen today anywhere else. Not even now in Florida."

So, how did it come to pass? That's what this book is about. That it was completed at all is due to many who shared their experiences. They know who they are. Most are quoted.

Special thanks to Earle Simpson, who conceived it; Bill Coy for initiating it; Ethel Furia for access to her voluminous files; Marion Reilly for use of her office equipment; Ken Leach for interpreting some tricky items and, especially, to Joe Tringali, whose early persistence helped slay the dragon.

Also to Elizabeth Whitney and the *St. Petersburg Times* for permission to reference her Cavanagh/Rotonda East article; and to Lang Capasso and the *Englewood Sun-Herald* for access to their morgue and to the *Sarasota Herald-Tribune* for permission to quote from articles and its vigilence in writing about the developer problems in the seventies.

Finally, to my capable editors and publishers, Linda and Jim Salisbury who asked good questions and were picky about details.

JACK ALEXANDER
Rotonda
June 1, 1994

Indians, Pirates and Predators

W HERE SHALL I BEGIN, your majesty?" he asked. "Begin at the beginning," the King said gravely, "and go on until you come to the end: then stop." So wrote Lewis Carroll in *Alice In Wonderland,* catching the essence of two problems with writing a history—where to begin, and when to stop.

Rotonda West began as a residential community in 1969, a year of epic, contrasting events. A whole generation became defined as 300,000 souls united in the mud of Woodstock and blew pot-smoke at the system; and Neil Armstrong's space boot stirred the dust on the moon, symbolizing forever man's determination to forge ahead into the unknown.

In that historic year, Rotonda West began to establish its niche on the map of Florida. Located on the West Coast in Charlotte County, Rotonda West is about halfway between Sarasota and Fort Myers.

Around the place that is now Rotonda swirls the sometimes violent folklore and history of Indians, Spanish conquistadors, pirates, predatory animals, land speculators and pioneers. And in more recent times those modern predators—land developers—who live only to use the land, for good or ill. The land—that is the real beginning.

The early days of the Rotonda land are best savored in the imagination—that the same scrub, palmetto, pines and ponds that now savage our golf scores once bore silent witness to the characters and events that shaped Florida itself.

The events, of course, include the Spanish invasion, the subsequent establishment of the state and its entry into the Union, and the state's decision to sell land as property—land on which Indians had run free.

For thousands of years in and around Rotonda, Calusa Indians raised their families and hunted and scavenged for shellfish along Coral Creek and around Charlotte Harbor. It is pleasurable to assume, even likely, that Indians once loped back and forth among their settlements across what are now the fairways and greenswards of Rotonda. Who can say otherwise?

The best known Florida Indians are the Seminoles. But old records are replete with tribe names: Aguacaleyquen, Potano, Tacobaga, Uzita, Apalachee, Tekesta, Timucuan, Creek, Miccosukee and Caloose (Calusa) among others.

It was the Calusa—and perhaps Timucuan—that roamed the Charlotte Harbor area. They are described in early records as sedentary, populous, tributary-fishing-and-hunting people. Their habitat was the southwest Florida coast down to Marco Island. They held sway in that productive estuarine environment from as early as 3,500 B.C. until the 17th century. It is well documented that Indians lived around nearby Lemon Bay for more than five thousand years.

Indeed, the Calusa kingdom in the mid-1500s numbered about fourteen thousand individuals, living in about seventy settlements and ruled by one the Spanish invaders called Carlos. Carlos, who was reputedly only six when he married his twelve-year-old bride, acceded to power around 1556 and spent much of his life fending off his northern (Tampa region) Indian rival Tocobaga.

But Carlos also had to resist foreign efforts to Christianize him and his people. In 1513, the late stages of the Calusa community, Florida was "discovered" by the Spaniard, Ponce de Leon. The Spanish adventurer sighted Florida while en route to Puerto Rico and landed, originally, on the East Coast. He thought it was an island and named it La Florida after a Spanish Easter feast. (Purists, of course, will point out that the English Cabot brothers, John and Sebastian, actually made Florida landfall as early as 1498. But they didn't follow up on their find.)

Ponce de Leon was later directed by the acquisitive King of Spain to colonize "the Isle of Florida." So, in 1521 he landed, this time in the vicinity of Charlotte Harbor, with two hundred men and fifty horses, and set about trying to establish a settlement in the area.

Along with Indians, then, we can place Spanish conquistadors in and around Rotonda, colonizing with their priests in the name of Christianity and killing all the Indians they could find.

Of their Indian opponents, the Spanish would report to their king, " . . . they occupy a very rocky and marshy country. The men go naked, the women in a shawl made of palm leaf. They are subjects of Carlos, and pay him tribute."

Ponce de Leon met with a hostile reception from the Indians, who were happy with their own gods. In fact, Carlos and his tribe didn't want foreigners messing with their heads or their habitat and, sedentary as they are described or not, they elected to do battle.

In one skirmish near Charlotte Harbor, according to one account, Ponce was wounded by a Calusa arrow, an injury from which he would later die in Cuba. It is said that he was mortally pierced in the thigh (some accounts say the buttocks, which may indicate that he was in retreat).

For his temerity, Carlos was executed by the Spaniards, who then proclaimed Carlos' son chief, giving him the name Don Pedro.

It is this Don Pedro for whom the spectacular island off Rotonda and Cape Haze is named, an island whose pristine beaches Rotonda and Cape Haze residents have rights to use in perpetuity—rights the early residents and potential lot buyers enjoyed, sometimes with noisy abandon as the original Cape Haze dwellers will attest.

More than one hundred years after Ponce de Leon, folk tradition says that another Spaniard, Hernando de Soto, arrived. There were other explorers, but de Soto brought an army of six hundred in nine ships, with horses and pigs which, a *Sarasota Herald-Tribune* historical account reports, " . . . didn't subtly meander through the terrain [but] swept across the countryside . . . ."

These foreign incursions ultimately decimated the Indians with war, and diseases which the Indians couldn't cope with. In time, the Calusa were driven from the Gulf Coast by the powerful Seminoles, first into the Everglades and then to Cuba.

Much of what is now Charlotte County was made an Indian reservation in the mid-1800s. In fact, President James Polk was forced to set aside a twenty-mile strip of land near Charlotte Harbor as a buffer between the Indian reservation and the increasing numbers of homesteaders.

Florida's Indian period, therefore, goes back into the mists of time. Its Spanish period began with Ponce de Leon. That lasted—with one twenty-year glitch—until 1821.

The glitch came in 1763 when the Spanish, failing in their quest for mineral riches and tired of fighting Indians, ceded Florida to the British. These new invaders came and killed more Indians, warring in particular with the Seminoles.

In time, it seems, they all became disenchanted with Florida. The British returned it to the Spanish in 1783 and went home. The Spanish, failing to find wealth as they had in Mexico and Peru, also gave up in disgust and, in 1819, ceded Florida to President James Monroe and the United States.

But the Spanish and British left behind some other characters to people the legends of the region around Rotonda—pirates.

One pirate, the Spaniard José Gaspar, reportedly put his mark on the area by settling in Southwest Florida at nearby Boca Grande on Gasparilla Island, just offshore from the future Rotonda. He built a fort on the island to house his female prisoners, but later moved them to an island further south he named Captiva, after its function.

It is claimed that Don José gave Gasparilla Island its name. It is also claimed that the island is named for Friar Gaspar, a Spanish missionary priest who ministered around Boca Grande. One takes one's pick. Both stories may be apocryphal, but they do romance the area's history.

Local legend has it that José Gaspar named Captiva, Sanibel, Cayo Costa and Useppa (formerly Josepha) where romanticists believe he hid one of his copper-lined treasure chests.

Gaspar was said to be a literate man from a good family. According to Jack Beater, author of *Pirates and Buried Treasure*[1], Gaspar rose to Admiral in the Spanish navy, but fled the court of King Charles III to avoid a scandal linking him with the Sicilian wife of Spain's crown prince.

To get away, Gaspar stole a ship. He became a pirate and forever nursed a hatred of Spain. Beater writes—in a book his publisher says is more myth and folklore than fact—that Gaspar cruised the Caribbean out of Boca Grande, looting a recorded thirty-six Spanish vessels over a twenty-six-year period.

What is neither myth nor folklore is an account from *American Monthly* magazine (February 1824) recounting an attack on the *Mary Anders*. This innocent vessel was overwhelmed in June 1820 by brigands under Gaspar's command.

The attackers swarming the *Mary Anders* were led by " . . . a wretch, shaggy whiskers covering nearly his whole face . . . who came at me, a naked cutlass in his fist, with which he struck me, knocking me down, blood running in torrents from my forehead," said a survivor.

But Gaspar eventually reached too far. In 1822 he set upon a vessel he thought was a British merchantman. It was a United States frigate, which blew Gaspar's ship out of the water—and Gaspar into it. He wrapped an anchor chain about his waist and plunged to a watery grave.

Boca Grande was also home for a while to Brewster Baker, an Englishman who joined up with José Gaspar and became " . . . one of Gasparilla's gang [whose] favorite hunting ground was the Gulf of Mexico," wrote Beater.

Baker was a former British navy officer who, having led a mutiny, turned to piracy and was befriended by Gaspar. Beater relates that Baker established a shore camp on nearby Pine Island and fell in with the notorious French pirate Pierre La Fitte, brother of bloodthirsty Jean La Fitte of New Orleans.

Baker is said to have stolen $12 million in gold from the Louisiana Purchase and buried it on Cape Haze. It could rest, conceivably, beneath the third green on The Links, or under a Windward residence— perhaps Fred and Peggy Winch's house, or George and Carol Frey's patio home, or the Cape Haze mansion of Bob and Regis Gorenflo. Who can say not, without digging?

Baker eventually left Florida for greener pastures (probably Cartagena) around 1820, but history records show that he died along the way, as had Ponce de Leon, struck by a poisoned Indian arrow. Unlike de Leon, however, Baker took his arrow in the chest.

The general area of Rotonda and its surrounds, then, including Coral Creek, Buck Creek, Lemon Bay, Grove City, El Jobean, Placida—and the reaches of Charlotte Harbor and Gasparilla, Don Pedro and the other barrier islands—were habitat to Indians, pirates and other predators long before homesteaders moved in.

When President James Monroe accepted Florida from Spain, he named Andrew Jackson the first governor. Two years later Tallahassee became the territory capitol. Florida joined the Union as the twenty-seventh state in 1845.

By then, pioneer homesteaders were struggling to survive this cruel land. Although it was a state, Florida was still a frontier wilderness and remained so until the early 1900s.

Settlers seeking to avoid the uncertainties of life in early Georgia and the Carolinas came to Florida, many determined to escape the pending Civil War. Those who were issued land permits through the Armed Forces Occupation Act came to the South with hope, but many couldn't cope with the hardships of Florida.

These hardships are described through the experience of a fictional family in the delightful novel, *A Land Remembered,* by Floridian Patrick Smith[2]. Smith recounts that in one year permits were issued that moved over six thousand settlers into virtually unknown, uncharted areas of Florida. There they were exposed to predatory animals and to the remaining Indians, who resented this new encroachment on their land. Many of the permits were annulled when the settlers caved in to Florida's harshness.

However, despite the cruel nature of Florida then, a hard core of pioneering communities eventually extended from Indian River and Tampa Bay south, down the Gulf Coast. They survived the cruelty of scrub and swamp, alligators, wild pigs that could snap a man's leg like a dry twig, panthers and bobcats, bears, wolves, rattlesnakes and other predators that roamed the peninsula and shared its unspoiled wildness with the Indians. And, of course, the ubiquitous mosquitoes, vicious enough when swarming to cause cattle to stampede. That, then, was the beginning.

In Rotonda, if you close your eyes, you can visualize the rawness of the early land, a file of helmeted Spaniards traversing the palmetto clumps, Carlos glowering at the invaders, a tri-masted pirate ship rocking at anchor off Cape Haze.

In a lighter vein, Congress, in 1987, reacted to our real or imagined latent feelings of guilt and passed the Indian Gaming Regulatory Act. This required states to give Indians rights to operate commercial gambling casinos on what was hitherto tribal land.

Imagine the consternation if descendants of Carlos today staked claim to Rotonda's twenty-six thousand acres, on grounds the land was stolen from their Calusa ancestors three hundred years ago.

A Calusa casino in the Rotonda hub. Outlandish? Look what a handful of Paugussetts have done in Connecticut, what the Mashantuckett Pequots are doing today in Bridgeport, and what the Seminoles have done in nearby Immokalee as recently as February, 1994.

Such are the vagaries of both myth and history.

Land For Sale

VENTUALLY THE been either eliminated or incarcerated. With the Treaty of 1821 with Spain, the United States had acquired Florida. Then, Congressional Acts approved in 1845 brought Florida into the Union. All public lands in Florida were now government property.

The move began to encourage private ownership of land—land on which Indians had once roamed free. In 1850, the Swamp Lands Act (an accurately descriptive title in parts of Florida) conveyed rights to sell or assign these lands to the state.

In 1855, Florida's legislature moved to "provide for and encourage a liberal system of internal improvements in the state," by vesting state land in five trustees: The Trustees of The Internal Improvement Fund of The State.

These gentlemen had the power and authority to sell wilderness land, including the twenty-six thousand acres now known as Rotonda.

The first sale of Rotonda land was recorded in 1885, to the Gainesville, Ocala and Charlotte Harbor Railroad. The company later became the Florida Southern Railway Company, and the deed was recorded in that name. As historians know, deeds, abstracts and early records do not always tell the entire story of land transactions, but they are one account.

The deed, dated May 13 of that year, was filed in Manatee County where, at the time, the Rotonda land was situated. In 1887 Manatee was divided, creating DeSoto County, and the land sale records were transferred to DeSoto in October 1888. There would be no Charlotte County for another thirty-three years.

The Rotonda land sale to the railroad was conditional. For each mile of railway built the company would get ten thousand acres.

The initial sale covered the land in areas now known as Rotonda's Heights, Lakes, Sands, Shores, Windward, and the strip on State Road 775 down to Fiddler's Green, including Sandalhaven and Gasparilla Pines.

Most of the land on the Cape Haze peninsula was parceled in forty- to eighty-acre lots. It changed hands frequently in the late 1800s, as speculation became rife.

In 1895, the railroad sold parcels in what is now Oakland Hills, Pebble Beach and Pine Valley to C. F. Adams of Duval County and to Jacob and Juliana Edwards of Boston, Massachusetts. This was the first individual ownership of Rotonda land to be recorded. Little is known about the first owners, but they soon lost the land for reasons unknown, most likely unpaid taxes.

In these years many land sales were ownership transfers resulting from tax forfeiture, though taxes then were as low as twenty-five cents an acre.

Swaps, sales and other consignments had Rotonda parcels at one time owned by Florida Commercial Company, L. N. Wilkie, and a DeSoto County land agent and speculator named John Cross. Cross was an energetic land promoter. Some accounts have him at Chicago expositions selling citrus groves in Grove City.

Many land transactions then were for amounts ranging from one dollar to seven hundred-twelve dollars, title records indicate.

In 1905, Albert W. Gilchrist—a portly Punta Gorda resident with a flowing mustache—became a land owner in what is now Rotonda. In 1909 Gilchrist, who died in 1926, became governor of Florida. Known for his business acumen and his generous will, he left his entire estate to charity. In recent years, State Rep. Vernon Peeples helped memorialize Gilchrist's governmental tenure and relationship to Charlotte County by having a waterfront park in Punta Gorda renamed Gilchrist Park. A span of the U.S. 41 bridge, completed in 1976, which connects Punta Gorda with Charlotte Harbor, is also named for Gilchrist. And of course there is also Gilchrist County in northern Florida.

Then, in 1908, President Teddy Roosevelt, who fished in Charlotte Harbor, established the Island Bay National Wildlife Refuge in Cape Haze.

Part of the land Gilchrist acquired came from the holdings of Cross and Wilkie, for which he paid four hundred dollars. He bid for more Rotonda area land at auction, specifically land seized by Sheriff A.C. Freeman of DeSoto County for non-payment of taxes and "sold at public auction in front of the courthouse door in Arcadia." Gilchrist's fifty-dollar bid was the highest.

Gilchrist purchased the balance of his Rotonda acres from Florida Commercial Co. for one dollar "and other considerations." He appears to have held this land until his death.

Before he died, spirited litigation was recorded between Gilchrist and White Beach Fruit Company over ownership of Rotonda and neighboring land. This company had bought its Rotonda acreage in 1924, from one J. A. Hendry, for $12,000 ($750 earnest money up front, $3,250 when the deed was furnished, and $8,000 over the next two years, with 8 percent semi-annual interest on any unpaid balance), according to records.

The land in question included eighty acres in Rotonda Heights around Sweetwater and Sunrise drives, one hundred eighty acres in adjoining Pebble Beach, forty acres in Broadmoor, and eighty acres in Pine Valley.

The squabble over ownership of the land was dismissed by Judge George Whitehurst of the Charlotte County Circuit Court, in November 1925. His ruling was appealed in March 1926. Gilchrist died shortly thereafter at age sixty-eight, but the suit was resubmitted in September 1926, against Gilchrist's executor, National Bank of Jacksonville. Judge Whitehurst rejected the appeal, and his ruling was upheld a year later by the Florida Supreme Court, in Tallahassee.

In accordance with the former governor's will, his land holdings, including "certain real and personal holdings situate in Charlotte County," went to the Masonic Home of Florida. This munificent bequest was joyfully accepted in 1931 by Leroy Brandon, grand master of the Most Worshipful Grand Lodge of Free and Accepted Masons.

Ten years after gratefully accepting the land bequest, the Masonic Home sold its Rotonda holdings to Morse Real Estate Corporation. Morse subsequently also acquired the balance of the land still held by White Beach Fruit Company.

There were, of course, other Rotonda land-holders. Frank Lewis of Philadelphia in 1887 and Mellon Drew of Duval County in 1892 acquired Rotonda parcels. Lewis had part of the St. Andrews segment of Rotonda and a portion of Oakland Hills as well as much of what is now Fiddler's Green and Wildflower. Lewis's plans for the land changed when his wife died in 1903 and he sold it to Southern Investment Company, a Delaware Corporation.

Corporations, in fact, were now becoming more involved as land prices soared beyond the reach of many individuals.

By now, Southern Investment Company's land holdings were a vast 98,500 acres, including the part of Rotonda they got from widower Lewis. Lewis, who had paid $4,000 for his Rotonda parcels, sold out six years later for $25,000, a 600 percent profit.

Southern Investment Company used the land to raise capital, first a $474,000 mortgage from International Trust Co. of Maryland, later a second mortgage of $500,000 from Fidelity Trust Co.

In 1917 they sold the land to Manasota Land & Timber Company, who immediately took a $650,000, 6 percent first mortgage from New York's Equitable Trust Co. The mortgage was later increased to $750,000 and assigned to Atlantic Trust Co. of Maryland.

The Manasota firm's interest, needless to say, was timber. They held the land and cleared much of it until 1925, when they sold 6,280 mostly Rotonda acres to Wilber Carter, of Greensboro, North Carolina, subject to a timber rights lease given to Gress Manufacturing Company.

This sale, however, involved a $115,000 mortgage held by the company, to be paid in three equal notes of $38,377 plus interest at 6 percent. This mortgage would eventually become a contentious issue among several future Rotonda land speculators.

Having made the deal with Manasota Land Company on December 29, 1924, Carter was quick to turn around and sell it, January 8, 1925, to a group of Florida investors who were incorporated as Intermediary Finance Corporation.

The price agreed upon was $314,000, but was subject to Carter's mortgage payable to Manasota Land Company. Other than that, the transaction called for a payment of $5,000 at signing and $193,866 in cash upon delivery of the deed. The agreement was formally closed May 5, 1925.

The investors immediately entered into an agreement to sell part of the land to Samual Lanski of Chicago for $7,500 up front, then $177,990 in four equal payments over four years. The price was based on $150 an acre.

As it turned out, for whatever reason, Lanski failed to come up with the cash, and four months later both sides abrogated the deal.

These property transfers left intact the railroad's right-of-way and the timber rights granted to Manasota Land & Timber Company and Gress Manufacturing Company. In 1924, in fact, the Gress firm had licensed G. W. Tuten of Georgia and W. S. Yearwood of Polk County "to cut and remove from said premises all timber measuring eight inches or more in diameter at a point eighteen inches above the ground, standing or growing on said land."

These "said premises" include much of what is now Oakland Hills, Pebble Beach, The Heights, St. Andrews, The Shores and Pine Valley, as well as the strip to Fiddler's Green.

The agreement with Gress required Tuten and Yearwood to complete, by March 1, 1924, "a sawmill of 150,000 feet per month or upwards, and by May 1, 1924, a sawmill of 300,000 feet per month or upwards." The lumber produced was to be sold to Gress Manufacturing "paid for at a rate of six dollars per thousand feet."

Wilbur Carter's $115,000 mortgage with Manasota Land Company cropped up again in 1927, when the company assigned it to Frank D. Frazier of Palm Beach. No more was heard of it until February 1935, when a lawsuit was filed by a Florida entity called Frazstate against Intermediary Finance Corporation et al, for relief through foreclosure of that mortgage.

The suit was filed in Charlotte County Circuit Court. The "et al" turned out to include F. L. Morse, along with H. H. Westinghouse, George H. Olney, Alwyn Ball, Jr., Walter Condict, and several executors of the late George Comstock's will.

Various legal actions and counteractions were filed in this suit during 1935. A final decree was issued, at last, by Judge Whitehurst, that required the Intermediary group to pay the outstanding portion of Carter's old $115,000 mortgage, namely $38,377 of unpaid principal and $22,600 in interest, plus court costs, plus an additional $4,000 to Frazstate for its legal fees. Where Wilbur Carter was during all this is a mystery.

The judge also decreed that, "in default of said payment being made the said mortgaged premises . . . will be sold . . . at public auction for cash in hand to the highest bidder, at the front door of the courthouse in Punta Gorda."

The group appears to have defaulted. On November 4, 1935, the sale of the land took place. This undeveloped scrub land, much denuded from timber stripping, and much of which is now Rotonda and its subdivisions—land that so many had desired, acquired, swapped, sold, or lost—finally wound up with Morse Real Estate Corporation, highest bidder at $25,000.

Morse apparently held most of the land until December 11, 1951. In that significant year, President Harry S. Truman fired General Douglas MacArthur as Far East commander, the United States signed a peace treaty with Japan, and two Vanderbilt brothers bought much of the land that subsequently became Rotonda, to make it into a ranch.

The Vanderbilts: Alfred and William

T HE VANDERBILT BROTHERS were direct descendants of the renowned Cornelius Vanderbilt. The name is a derivation of Vander Bilt, belonging to Dutch farmers mostly, who settled in and around New York, in Brooklyn and Staten Island.

The "Commodore," as Cornelius was known, was a fur trader, ferry boat captain and financier. He was an active and successful businessman who made his fortune relatively late in life as a railroad financier, helping to found the New York Central Railroad.

Cornelius came by the gratuitous title the "Commodore," for his early shipping activities, starting with one ship plying between Man-

3.1 Aerial view of the original Cape Haze community developed by the Vanderbilt brothers.

hattan and Staten Island, forerunner of the famous Staten Island ferry of today. A crusty gentleman, he is alleged to have told a competitor, "You have undertaken to cheat me. I won't sue you, for the law is too slow. I'll ruin you."

Commodore Vanderbilt died at eighty-three, leaving in excess of $100 million, having started his unique family down its long road to American business and financial success.

The Commodore's son, William Henry, was equally blunt. He is remembered as saying, to a persistent reporter dogging him with questions about his business affairs who had the temerity to suggest the public's right to know, "The public be damned."

A later Vanderbilt, Harold, was reputedly a contract bridge genius, for whom the Vanderbilt Club—the card-playing premises in New York and the bridge convention—was named; and for his passion for racing yachts. He successfully defended The America's Cup on three occasions in the 1930s against Sir Thomas Lipton of British tea fame.

Another Vanderbilt, Alfred, was lost at sea when the ocean liner *Lusitania* was torpedoed during World War I.

Vanderbilts were rich, famous, successful in many fields and well known long before the name turned up in connection with Rotonda.

In 1951, Alfred's son, William, of Williamstown, Massachusetts, was driving with his wife, Anne around Florida.

One of the first people the Vanderbilts talked to in Charlotte County was then County Agent N.H. ("Doc") McQueen in his upstairs office in the courthouse. They were interested in information on agriculture and cattle ranching. "Doc" McQueen spent much time with William who was the managing partner of the land the brothers purchased. "Doc" worked with and advised the Vanderbilts on the development of the 2-V ranch. Later he got watermelon farmers to clean the pine and palmetto land, then improved the pastures with bahia and pangola grass for ranch cattle.

Rotonda land at the time was a virtual wasteland of scrub, pine, palmetto and marsh. *Perfect for ranching*, William thought. (At least the part that wasn't too wet.)

He persuaded his half-brother, Alfred, of Jericho, New York, to join him in purchasing it and establishing 2-V Ranch.

They paid $700,000 (about twenty dollars an acre) taking an initial mortgage of $250,000, with annual payments of $12,500 to be made every June until 1971, to Travelers Insurance Company. Court documents indicate that the mortgage was fully paid by February 20, 1967.

They would buy additional acreage in October 1958, bringing their Rotonda area holdings to 35,033 acres. They would later sell off about 10,000 acres, at the northern end of the property flanking State Road 775, to General Development Corporation, getting a juicy four hundred dollars an acre on their twenty-dollar-an-acre investment.

According to the *Sarasota Herald-Tribune*, December 12, 1951, the Vanderbilt purchase was "the largest land deal in Charlotte County in twenty years, and the largest ever on the Coast."

Over the next two decades, the 2-V ranch flourished as the Vanderbilts improved it. It was, on the one hand, a playground where the brothers entertained their friends from up north. On occasion they would stay at the venerable Gasparilla Inn in nearby Boca Grande.

On the other hand, the ranch was for serious cattle breeding. William already had a substantial registered dairy herd up north. The brothers wanted to develop Santa Gertrudis cattle, a breed tough enough to survive the rigors peculiar to Florida (weather, mosquitoes) yet provide choice quality beef.

To this end they purchased one hundred (some records say one thousand) cows and one lucky bull. The cattle were special stock, crossbred from Hereford (for meat) and Brahma (for strength). The brothers brought in a fellow named Owen Keene as foreman of 2-V ranch. Keene came from the A.C. Frizzell ranch in Murdock when the 2-V ranch purchased 1,000 head. He drove them across an old wooden bridge at El Jobean.

Historian Vernon Peeples, who knew William, said that the Vanderbilts gave twelve miles of road between El Jobean and Placida to Charlotte County in exchange for a fence on one side of the road to keep their cattle in.

"I knew the Vanderbilts very well," said attorney Leo Wotitzky. "We represented them when they acquired the land . . . and I formed the Cape Cave Corporation for them." Wotitzky also handled the sale of ten thousand acres to General Development. "That was mostly their bull pasture," he said.

Wotitzky remembers William as an unpretentious, friendly individual, although he was a director of the New York Central Railroad (he would never fly) and governor of Rhode Island. Alfred, after a naval career, was a sportsman, interested particularly in race horses and active in the Thoroughbred Breeders Association and president of the New York Racing Commission. He owned "Native Dancer."

"They were both pretty friendly guys," Wotitzky said of the Vanderbilts. The veteran Punta Gorda lawyer recalls visiting Alfred in New York, and being taken into the starter's box at Belmont where he could look down on the horses before the race.

"I asked him which one I should bet on," Wotitzky said.

"I don't bet and I don't give any advice," was Vanderbilt's retort.

"So I bet anyway," said Wotitzky. "I lost."

Charlotte County rancher, banker and developer, Robert N. ("Bucky") McQueen describes Alfred and William as tall, distinguished-looking and well-spoken.

During their years on the Cape the Vanderbilts dabbled with their ranch. Alfred built a house in Cape Haze. William acquired a large tract of Gulf-front property on Manasota Key, where he had a winter estate.

They began to improve the Rotonda land for cattle pasture and develop Cape Haze as a rather high-class residential subdivision, through their Cape Cave Corporation. The Vanderbilts brought in an old navy friend of Alfred's, Jim Costigan, to later head their real estate development. Costigan was a congenial fellow according to Roger Mashke, present owner of Radio Shack in Englewood, who shared a frequent drink with him.

Among the early Cape Haze residents were Lil Klatt and her husband, who came to the area from Toledo, Ohio. They bought a lot from the Vanderbilts in 1956, but they did not build on it until 1964.

"The Rotonda area was pretty much a swamp then," Lil Klatt recalls, "but I wanted to live here in Cape Haze and nowhere else. I wanted to be cremated and thrown into Pelican Bay."

Klatt says she never did meet the Vanderbilts in all the years she was down here. "They weren't here very often, although William came down more than Alfred did."

Leo Wotitzky remembers it the same way. "William spent a good bit of time down here, but Alfred wasn't down that much," he said. "I think William became a resident of Florida but Alfred never did."

As the fifties gave way to the sixties, the economics of the area were becoming more pronounced. The Vanderbilts awarded oil and gas exploration, prospecting, drilling and mining leases on the land to several companies, including Magnolia Petroleum of Dallas, Texas, which was acting for Mobil Oil Company and the California Company, representing Socony Mobil Oil Company. No oil or gas was ever discovered although drilling was done east of State Road 771.

They also allowed easements to Florida Power and Light, "to set and maintain poles, guy stubs, wires and anchors for electric transmission and distribution lines . . . and to trim and keep clear all trees, brush and undergrowth that might endanger said lines."

The Vanderbilts also formed Cape Haze Water Company, Inc., of Placida, Florida. It would become Rotonda West Utility Company in 1972, two years after Rotonda West was launched, and, later, a subsidiary of Rotonda Properties, Inc., in 1980. As shall be seen, the water company would figure in a mortgage foreclosure battle between the Vanderbilts and the original developers of Rotonda West.

They then sold an easement to their own Cape Haze Water Company for a pipeline. This was a strip of land two hundred fifty feet wide running essentially from Buck Creek, through parts of Pebble Beach, Oakland Hills, Windward, and Cape Haze East. Its track stayed east of the west shore of Coral Creek and ended at the Coral Creek dam.

The Vanderbilts installed the dam at the northeast corner of Windward to keep the salt water side of the creek from going north and for use as potable water.

Needing potable water for the ranch, the Vanderbilts set down various wells but found they were pulling salt water, according to Galen Custard, who would later administer the utility for Rotonda. Interestingly enough, these wells could never be located after the Vanderbilts left the area.

"They were somewhere in Cape Haze East, but we're not sure where," Custard said. "The only way we know they existed is that some of the Albritton family remember them. The water lines also served the fishery operation at Placida." Ms. Albritton owned The Fishery. Now her sons do.

In their days, the Vanderbilts did not have government permits to worry about. They could put down wells where they chose, Custard pointed out. When their wells turned salty, they simply relocated their wellfield to where it is today, along Boundary Boulevard, catty-corner to the Riverhouse Condominium complex.

The Vanderbilts showed a good deal of foresight, Galen Custard suggested. "It would have been more difficult to find fresh water around here without that dam. The Vanderbilts did a lot of good things. The [later] developers [of Rotonda] probably did more damage than the Vanderbilts did good."

On February 2, 1967, with their mortgage virtually cleared, William and Anne sold most of their Rotonda holdings to brother Alfred.

By now the land was more desirable as developable acreage, making the economics of beef difficult. The Vanderbilts had been trying to sell the ranch for ten years at $9.5 million. Then, after one week of a bidding war between Joe Klein and another company, on September 6, 1969, Alfred sold the ranch to Cavanagh Leasing Corporation of Miami for $19.5 million. The Cape Cave Corporation became a wholly owned Cavanagh subsidiary.

William Vanderbilt died in 1981 at his Cricket Creek farm in Williamstown, Massachusetts. His obituary, carried locally, said he had been popular in the area, active in the community, and a major contributor to local schools.

Two short months after United States astronaut Neil Armstrong stood on the surface of the moon, Rotonda was put on the map of Florida, and would acquire, subsequently, something of a reputation at home and abroad.

Along Came Joe Klein

IF ROTONDA HAD been square, perhaps fewer would have come. A round community is romantic. It conjures up visions of wagon trains in their nightly comfort circles. Round is soft, like Paris. No hard edges, like square New York.

Rotonda was said to have been the vision of one Charles Prynne Martin, a man alleged to lack formal architectural or land planning credentials. Martin likened his radial design to Washington, D.C. and Paris, saying, "spiritual guidance alone conceived its creation."

Martin's vision was embraced by a smallish, slender man named Joe Klein. In old photos he looked a bit like the late actor George Raft, without Raft's trademark fedora.

"Yes, I met Joe Klein," said Ed Hennessey, a Rotonda West resident who would become president of the Rotonda West Property Owners Association in 1987. "Tricky Joe . . . he was shrewd. I'm a small person in stature, but Klein was littler than I am," Hennessey said.

Klein reportedly dropped out of college at the University of Pittsburgh to help the family real estate business when his father became ill. Later, bored selling television service contracts, he moved to Florida and got into land sales with Gulf American Land Corporation, a company renowned for selling land like cans of beans, using what one writer described as "boiler-room phone selling and sweat-box closing techniques."

Selling land was Klein's niche. He took to land selling like a duck to a swamp, to use an apt analogy, and was suave, articulate and likable. He quickly formed his own firm, World Wide Realty, which became a sales agent for Gulf American. Klein then moved through several corporate relationships where the business usually involved the sale of

Florida land. In time, he formed Palm Beach Investment Properties as a subsidiary to his principle corporate entity, Cavanagh, and within a few years his business reportedly had annual sales of around $12 million.

Cavanagh Mercantile Corporation was incorporated in Delaware in 1964, became Cavanagh Leasing Corporation in 1968, and then consolidated into Cavanagh Communities Corporation in 1970. The corporate name change was appropriate. The company was then launching Rotonda West, a new community.

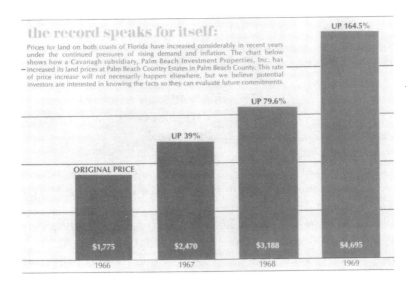

the record speaks for itself:

Prices for land on both coasts of Florida have increased considerably in recent years under the continued pressures of rising demand and inflation. The chart below shows how a Cavanagh subsidiary, Palm Beach Investment Properties, Inc. has increased its land prices at Palm Beach Country Estates in Palm Beach County. This rate of price increase will not necessarily happen elsewhere, but we believe potential investors are interested in knowing the facts so they can evaluate future commitments.

UP 164.5%

UP 79.6%

UP 39%

ORIGINAL PRICE

| $1,775 | $2,470 | $3,188 | $4,695 |
| 1966 | 1967 | 1968 | 1969 |

4.1 Artist's conception of Rotonda's commercial core which cost $40,000 to build. Banned from use in the sales of Rotonda East, it was much used in the sales of Rotonda West.

Before that, in the mid-sixties, Klein began to sell the original Rotonda on the East Coast, on land that straddled the border between Martin and Palm Beach counties. According to the sales pitch of the time, Rotonda East was to be a city-in-the-round of fifty thousand.

From his prior experience, Klein had to be familiar with land sales techniques then prevailing in Florida. These were the days of "Buyer Beware" in Florida land sales, an unseemly business sometimes called "swamp peddling," to quote the *St. Petersburg Times*. Developers would acquire cheap swamp or wet land, put in some roads, divide the land into salable lots, price them up to twenty times their cost, then sell them aggressively on the basis of their future in a "sunshine community."

Florida had a long history with such land sales from the 1800s, the 1920s and the 1950s. After World War II, the Florida boom began, with the developers of South Venice and Harbour Heights perfecting the sales techniques which were later employed by other developers, according to Vernon Peeples.

Techniques included selling plots that were never surveyed, or even staked, often on a "sight-unseen" basis. Many buyers learned, usually too late, that their land was partially submerged, couldn't be developed, sometimes couldn't even be found.

"You mean you bought some Florida land . . . ?" became the basis for jokes told all over the world, to the amusement of everyone except those who lost both dignity and money doing just that.

It wasn't until the late 1960s that land sales regulation brought order to what had been a wild, speculative business, one that enriched many but also financially damaged thousands.

Florida's reputation for questionable land sales practices in the fifties and sixties was well earned, and Rotonda East undoubtedly contributed to it. Photos of the Rotonda East site taken as late as 1972 show it as a swamp without a house on it.

In 1966, with the birth of Rotonda East, Klein's aggressive sales machine sold 7,500 acres in Palm Beach County and 10,000 acres in Martin County, Florida, at prices variously reported up to $4,500 per lot, in some cases as high as $6,000 per acre and a quarter, for land selling a few years earlier for $300 an acre.

This new community, Rotonda East, was to be developed according to Charles Martin's radial concept. It would be a glamorous circular city with marinas, broad navigable canals, golf courses and zoning for both residential and commercial use.

At first, the project was applauded by county authorities. But their applause turned to concern as unappetizing aspects of the development began to come to light and Klein was unable to get the permits.

In a 1972 article in the *St. Petersburg Times*, real estate and urban development writer Elizabeth Whitney reported that the Florida Land Sales Board had earlier denied renewal of Klein's sales registration, "because of his past sales activities." Whitney's comprehensive article provided many insights into Klein's early land sales career.

The particular activities with which the state took issue included persuading potential buyers to sign blank installment contracts and showing multi-colored brochures without supporting property reports, which are now familiar as public offering statements. After years of apparent indifference, state law finally prohibited the practice in 1964.

Why anyone would sign a blank contract, of course—like signing a blank check—is beyond most of us, yet many did, and lived to regret their foolishness.

Moreover, selling the sizzle without revealing the steak apparently didn't stop, even after August 1, 1967, when more detailed new state land-sales regulations became law. General Development Corporation, a major developer in Charlotte County (and elsewhere in the state) faced the legal music some years later on this score.

As for Rotonda West, questionable sales tactics, mainly misrepresentation, would become one basis later for a veritable flood of complaints and litigation involving the sale of that property. Much of this might have been avoided had the experiences of Rotonda East buyers been known.

In her article about Rotonda East, Elizabeth Whitney quoted a Martin County official: "We had to stop discussion on Rotonda. While they were dealing with us in open session, they were selling and wheeling and dealing behind our backs."

Many Rotonda East property buyers eventually queried the pace of construction of amenities and infrastructure in their new community. According to Whitney, "replies from the courthouse were that there was no construction, and that much of the land was under water and was assessed at $1,400 an acre."

Meanwhile, in the late 1960s, a new word was being drummed into public awareness—ecology. And about 1962, Charlotte County adopted its first building and zoning code.

Plans for Rotonda East came under the critical scrutiny of a new wave of social critics concerned about, of all things, the environment. Whitney noted that the stated intent to drain Rotonda East into the St. Lucie Canal didn't go down well with the environmentalists. Nor did the piling into a county of twenty-eight thousand people of Rotonda's anticipated fifty thousand make for sound mathematics, particularly for the affluent residents in nearby Stuart, Whitney reported.

Rotonda East's drainage plan was eventually rejected by the U.S. Army Corps of Engineers. The zoning boards and commissions of both Palm Beach and Martin counties allied against Rotonda East. According to press reports, Klein was accused in one international incident of continuing to sell Rotonda East land on the basis of its drainage plan, without revealing that the plan had been officially rejected.

Over time, publicity for Rotonda East became more and more negative. A Pratt-Whitney engineer told writer Elizabeth Whitney that the development's proximity to his plant's engine test site would make homes there "virtually uninhabitable." Residents were not told "they would be living . . . almost constantly . . . with a noise . . . like hearing an airplane at one thousand feet, or the screech of a train whistle at two hundred yards," to quote Whitney's article.

4.2 Impressive statistics appealing to potential investors were widely used in the selling of Rotonda lots.

Among the tools used for selling Rotonda East was a twenty-one foot-diameter scale model of the proposed project, built at a reported cost of $40,000. It was so perfectly to life it even included tiny cars on its streets. It depicted roads, canals and houses, golf courses and marinas. It was wired to light up and looked for all the world like a city rolling by beneath a landing airplane.

The model was wired to work in conjunction with a huge wall mural. A salesman could illuminate on the model any point of interest on the mural.

According to Whitney, Land Sales Board investigators once paid a surprise visit to Klein's Palm Beach sales office. Afterwards, because the model had no relationship with the reality of the project, they ordered it banished to an inner room remote from sales activity. However, brash Cavanagh salesmen, conscious of their commissions, still would sneak potential buyers "furtively" into the back room for a "secret" peek—which usually clinched their sale.

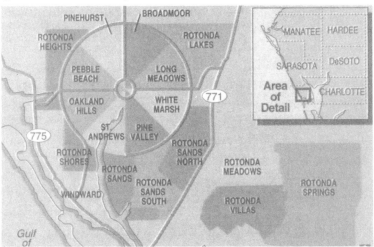

4.3 Overview of the plan of the Rotonda development showing the location of the subdivisions inside and outside the "wheel." (Reprinted from the *Sarasota Herald-Tribune.* ©1994. All rights reserved.)

Elizabeth Whitney, now retired from the *St. Petersburg Times*, related that Klein and his people learned that she was researching for an in-depth article on his business dealings. She said Klein requested a meeting with the editor, Gene Paterson, who told him they could meet only if Whitney was also present.

"Klein arrived for the meeting with his lawyer and an engineer," Whitney said. "Besides the editor and me, the managing editor and the city editor were present. The seven of us sat on opposite sides of a long table in our conference room for a grueling two hours, after which the story—one of the longest ever run by the *Times*—was duly published."

Whitney spent three months researching Klein's early land sales operations, many of which were related to Rotonda East, although by November 1972, when the article appeared, Cavanagh had Rotonda West humming with activity through its Cape Cave subsidiary.

In the late 1960s, Klein's firm, which he headed with his Hungarian-born father, Zola, was known as Cavanagh Leasing Corporation. While he was pitching Rotonda East, he was using his glamorous "half-billion dollar, city-in-the-round" to promote two other swampy, unplatted properties: Palm Beach Country Estates and Palm Beach Heights. His claim was that they would benefit by their closeness to Rotonda East.

Rotonda East, of course, died stillborn.

But Cavanagh, by then, had achieved a certain prominence in land sales. The company had a wide ranging selling organization that went far beyond the professionals in forty-six sales agencies in major cities around the country and abroad. It seemed like every hotel, restaurant, tourist area and even parking lot in Florida had its Rotonda touts. These were waitresses, valet-parking attendents, swimming-pool lifeguards, taxi drivers and hotel receptionists. These amateur sales touts were slipped $10, $15 or $20 for every potential buyer they could steer to a Rotonda sales center or cocktail reception, where aggressive solicitations would take place.

Elizabeth Whitney reported that Cavanagh paid employees at one Miami hotel $1,730 in one month. The manager at another hotel received $100, with smaller payments going to the telephone operators, desk clerks and pool attendants.

Typical was the experience of George Perry, now a resident in the Pebble Beach subdivision in Rotonda West. Perry, a football coach from Michigan, came to Florida with an assistant in the mid-sixties to attend a College All-Stars football game at the Orange Bowl. They stayed at the ritzy Fountainbleau Hotel in Miami Beach and enjoyed a rousing night out after the game.

As Perry tells it, "The phone rang early the next morning. It was the hotel's social director asking if we'd like to tour a warship in Fort Lauderdale, then go inland and see some alligator wrestling."

Having no other plans, Perry accepted. He recalls that they were "tripped" (free transportation), and their limousine ultimately deposited them, at dusk, at a cocktail party at the Diplomat Hotel, where Perry quickly found himself signing installment sales contracts for several Rotonda lots.

Perry then returned home to Michigan, where, sometime later, "a salesman turned up at my door and tried to sell me more Rotonda lots," he said. Perry declined, having no thought at the time of ever moving to Florida. He eventually did, however, and exchanged two of the lots he had bought for his present Rotonda West property.

Earlier Rotonda West residents tell similar stories, many of which conjure up images of major U.S. cities swarming with Rotonda sales touts, exhibits at state fairs, champagne parties, free trips, prizes and all the hullabaloo of high pressure land selling for which Florida was still notorious, even after state regulations were stiffened.

Perry sold two other Rotonda lots twenty years later for a 400 percent profit.

Harry and Harriet Virtue, from Beach Haven, New Jersey, also bought several Rotonda West lots (in the Pinehurst subdivision). They still own them and claim they have appreciated five times. The Perry's and Virtue's investment experiences may be unique, however. Peripheral lots—especially outside the Rotonda West circle—are unlikely to increase that much, except, perhaps, in the long-term and depending on development progress.

Owners of such remote lots who took advantage of Cavanagh's offer to "exchange" them for lots in developed subdivisions usually found they had to pony up more cash. Some found, when they listed their lots for sale with area brokers, that the lots were worth only a fraction of what the owners had paid for them.

In the early 1970s Cavanagh sought a New York Stock Exchange listing to give the company credibility and provide access to more capital. The company reported it had "adequate financing . . . to make judicious use of our properties." The listing was granted in 1972, and Cavanagh became a NYSE member, a $138 million public company with 1,500 employees.

By then, of course, Cavanagh's development focus had moved to southwest Florida. Having had his Rotonda East spurned on the East Coast, Joe Klein learned of the Vanderbilt's desire to sell their Cape Haze property and decided it would make a perfect relocation for his Rotonda dream.

When it came here, Rotonda West was warmly welcomed by Charlotte County authorities, who either ignored or were unaware of the experiences their East Coast peers had with Cavanagh's method of operating.

All they could see was *The Vision* being presented. And, like many of the early buyers, they believed it would really come to pass—a bonanza, right in their own county.

The Rotonda Vision

I NEGOTIATED THE deal when the Vanderbilts sold their land to Cavanagh," said attorney Leo Wotitzky. "It's an interesting story. Joe Klein was a flamboyant kind of guy, a real promoter." Wotitzky, remember, had represented the Vanderbilts in the 1950s when they sold ten thousand acres of their original purchase to the Mackle brothers, whose General Development Corporation had developed Port Charlotte.

In 1969, Wotitzky was attending an annual meeting of the Vanderbilts' corporation at Cape Haze. Alfred offered him the real estate commission if he could sell the Vanderbilt ranch.

"He said I'd also get my attorney's fees, so I told him it sounded pretty interesting to me," Wotitzky said.

The now venerable Punta Gorda lawyer immediately began negotiations with several people, including Land Resources Corporation, developer of Lehigh Acres, a huge planned-development in neighboring Lee County.

"We got along pretty well with these negotiations," Wotitzky recalled. At one point he almost headed for New York with a proposal for the Vanderbilts, but it fell through at the last minute. "We were already on the plane," Wotitzky said. "Suddenly the other guy said something that killed the deal right then."

Wotitzky went back to square one, but, in time, he was able to negotiate with a Miami group and reach a tentative agreement on a sale price of around $10 million.

"I recommended to William and Alfred that they pursue the deal," Wotitzky continued. "They were considering it when suddenly, out of the blue, I had a telephone call from Joe Klein, whom I'd never heard of. He wanted to talk to me about the Vanderbilt property. Could he meet me at Cape Haze?"

As Wotitzky tells it, Joe Klein and some of his relatives had circled over the property by air. "That's all they did," he shrugged in disbelief, "looked at it from the air. They flew in, landed at the little air strip on [County Road] 771, came in, and made an offer. I don't recall the amount, but it was in excess of the offer we were considering from the other people. I told Klein I'd submit his offer to the Vanderbilts and tell them they had another prospective buyer."

On Friday June 13, 1969, a series of phone calls to Wotitzky began. "Both sides kept bidding and I'd pass each one the bids of the other," Wotitzky said (representing both sides in the transaction). "They'd increase each bid by about half a million. Klein finally bid it up to nineteen million. It was pretty exciting."

The deal was closed in New York two months later, the Vanderbilts taking back a mortgage of about $15 million, in effect financing the deal themselves. Subsequently, there would be "continuing issues" that came up between the parties, the largest being when Cavanagh later defaulted on part of the purchase-money mortgage.

After all, as Wotitzky pointed out, "Joe Klein had tried to put a development on the east coast. When he couldn't he just picked up these plans, brought them over here [to the Cape Haze peninsula] and adapted them to this site. They were a bunch of promoters and lived high while they had it."

Were they just a bunch of promoters? Or did Joe Klein really have a vision, one that gave way to reality due to mismanagement, economic constraints, and other circumstances?

Shangri-La was an idyllic place, but it existed only in James Hilton's famous novel, *Paradise Lost*. Camelot was legend, not reality. But Cavanagh salesmen were offering "Rotonda West: Sunlit gem in a perfect setting," supported by color brochures that surely excited the imagination.

There were two sales pitches, one on valuation to those interested in real estate investment for appreciation, the other on the Florida lifestyle, to retirees and others who were seeking constant sunshine, and the pleasures of golfing, sailing, fishing as potential residents.

5.1 Artist's portrayal of *The Vision* as it would look after completion.

To investors, Charlotte County was touted as "a leader in Florida's growing future." One Cavanagh brochure contained a chart that promised "fast-paced progress" on the order of a 555 percent increase in assessed property valuation since 1960, in "the second fastest growing county in the state."

Cavanagh quoted the *County Courier* which editorialized, "Florida will number more than 8.5 million by the end of the 1970s . . . a 40 percent growth." the *Courier* rhapsodized that this would mean "more money from the federal government for programs, more building, more businesses creating more jobs." Small print noted that the *Courier* was published by Palm Beach Investment Properties, a subsidiary of Cavanagh Leasing Corporation.

Three former U.S. presidents were quoted to bolster the sales pitch. One with "A message from Florida's Number One resident" over a picture of Richard Nixon, had Nixon saying, "The seventies will prove to be a decade of greatness for Florida." Grover Cleveland was quoted,

"No investment is so sure . . . so safe . . . so certain to enrich . . . as well-selected realty." Even Teddy Roosevelt was quoted as saying, " . . . real estate is the basis of all wealth."

An early Rotonda ad in *Florida Trend* and other magazines urged, "Choose the site now for your Florida home, purchase it in comfortable installments over a ten-year period. When paid for, the equity can be used in the original outlay required for building when you're ready. In eight short years, Florida land prices have increased nearly eighty percent."

Another brochure that promoted Rotonda West as an investment opportunity claimed a 16 percent increase in nationwide prices of land for homes per year. Opposite the claim was a bar chart showing that Cavanagh-owned land prices in Palm Beach County had increased 164.5 percent in the period 1966 to 1969.

A short-term gain of that magnitude appealed to thousands of investors in the United States and abroad. By 1970 Cavanagh's own annual report was crowing "approximately 3,000 acres have been sold . . . since the peninsula's acquisition for in excess of $70 million." The report credited "our highly effective sales organization for providing a ready-made marketing adjunct for Rotonda development."

One of Joe Klein's dreams had Rotonda West as part of "a megalopolis of the future." As conceived in Cavanagh sales literature this would stretch from Miami up the East Coast, arc across the state through Orlando to Tampa, then down the west coast to Naples . . . embracing Rotonda West on the way. This was the tangible opportunity Cavanagh was pitching to investors, noting that "where people go, real estate values grow."

One brochure projected Florida's growth by the year 2000 at an additional 6 million, citing the U.S. Census Bureau as the information source. The statistical information barrage continued with a Florida Chamber of Commerce prediction that "Next week 3,942 more people will move to Florida." Another brochure quoted a state senator as saying, with typical political abandon, "If Florida duplicates the growth of the last ten years we will surpass the combined population of Nevada, Alaska, Vermont, Wyoming and half of Delaware."

While potential lot purchasers were being enticed by the prospect of juicy profits, new residents were being lured to "a glittering choice of living styles . . . Rotonda West—sunlit gem in a perfect setting."

The public offering statement filed by Cavanagh's Cape Cave Corporation on November 3, 1969, said Rotonda West was "an area of 5,400 acres within the 26,000-acre Rotonda community and comprised 9,223 lots."

The Vision? Promotional material portrayed it as a brand new community-in-the-round, a unique circle of eight pie-slice-shaped subdivisions, seven with their own golf courses and marinas, the eighth with a broad waterway (Coral Creek). The whole would be surrounded by a circular waterway, offering, in all, "thirty-two miles of navigable, blue-green waterways well-stocked with freshwater fish."

Entry would be across four bridges, from north, south, east and west, each with its own security gate.

The seven eighteen-hole golf courses would be named for the days of the week. The 6,620 yard "championship" Sunday course (now The Hills) was built quickly, opening November 1971, as the first residents moved into their homes. The *Vision* proclaimed "a firm commitment from Cavanagh to complete six more courses before 1978"

An ad in *Florida Trend*, April 1972, said, "Here now are 20 miles of boulevards, streets, curbs and gutters completed or under construction . . . canals and recreational waterways . . . with 10 percent of the total planned 32 miles already completed. Here now are underground utility lines and full city conveniences . . . a magnificent 6620-yard, 18-hole championship golf course . . . with a firm commitment to complete six more golf courses and other recreational facilities by 1977."

When it was finished, the story went, Rotonda West would be a community of 60,000 people on 5,400 acres, living in ranch-style and split-level homes, each with its own swimming pool. (While the 60,000-person projection doesn't square with the stated 9,223 lots, these were the numbers variously presented).

Prices for houses would range from $22,100 to $36,300, excluding the lot, according to the Cape Cave price list. The eight subdivisions were Oakland Hills, Pebble Beach, Pinehurst, Broadmoor, Long Meadow, White Marsh, Pine Valley and St. Andrews.

And this was just within the circle. Outside the circle there were countless other lot sales opportunities. The Lakes: 2,863 lots and a 100 acre industrial park; Sands: two segments, one with 927 multi-family sites on 624 acres, the other with 6,011 single-family sites on 2,307 acres; Villas: 3,212 home sites, 51 commercial sites, lakes and parks;

Heights: 1,981 home sites, a 25-acre park, commercial lots; Shores: 617 home sites; Meadows: 2,362 single family home sites, 84 multi-family sites, 56 commercial sites. There also would be The Springs flanking Charlotte Harbor, and straddling Coral Creek, Windward and Cape Haze East.

Then there was the Cape Haze subdivision itself, already partially developed by the Vanderbilts, with attractive luxury homes in unusual bay, cove, and waterway settings. It included an existing nine-hole golf course, gun club, skeet range and cabana club. (Some Windward lots also had been sold previously by the Vanderbilts.)

Rotonda's residential lots would range in size from 7,500 square feet for single family to 196,000 square feet for multi-family. They were to be laid out with no homesite backing onto another. Each eventual homesite would overlook a canal, a golf course, a landscaped green belt, or a recreational waterway.

Bridges on the canal system promised to provide ten-foot clearance underneath and each canal would have a minimum six-foot water depth, making for "a recreational waterway for pleasure craft."

The "Vital Center" in the hub, zoned commercial, would contain, in its "ingeniously designed one hundred-acre core," tree-lined pedestrian esplanades, a park, stores, business and professional offices, a theater, and a circulating restaurant atop "a towering observation building rising from the center . . . [with] a fountain cascading into a crystal lake."

In fairness, most of the printed material contained small print warnings and qualifications, such as "although our canal system is not directly connected, the Intracoastal Waterway is only a mile away." In another, "this is a true architect's rendering . . . [but] . . . none of the buildings [in the hub] are planned or proposed at this time, and their construction is not the responsibility of the developer."

However, Joe Klein was quoted in the Palm Beach *Post-Times*, September 20, 1970, comparing his vision for Rotonda West to his failed dream, Rotonda East.

"The Palm Beach-Martin County site was land-locked," Klein said, "and would have required extensive excavation to allow boat travel to open water. We already have water access to the Gulf of Mexico here." (Klein may have been referring to the Capstan Canal in Cape Haze, which the Vanderbilts had built to provide Gulf access from there.)

Additional sales inducements: Rotonda's private beach on Don Pedro Island, access provided free by a corporate-operated ferry; subdivisions to have underground power lines and curbed streets (a promise kept only in Oakland Hills); General Electric and Hotpoint appliances in the homes (GE later had to deny claims that they were corporately involved in the development of Rotonda West); central water and sewage facilities.

What would turn out later to be a critical mistake by Cavanagh was to commit to completion of the basic infrastructure—paved streets, sewer lines, water lines, bridges, buried electrical conduits, and many of the amenities—by December 31, 1977. It wouldn't happen.

However, in January 1970, a surveyor jammed a stake in the ground and said, "This is it, fellows. The center of Rotonda West." And a community was born.

Birth of a Community

THE COMMUNITY of Rotonda West began with a population of three: Harry and Joan Kaar, and their son Jeff. The Kaars moved into their home, 8 Annapolis Lane, in October 1971.

Michael and Dorothy Saunders of Englewood had signed the first official Rotonda sales contract in 1969. Early residents still differ about who was first, second and third in residence. But the honor of being first goes to the Kaars, followed two weeks later by Minnesotans Ed and Billie Dodds, then the Saunders—such as the records are.

As to it being an honor to be Resident Number One, Joan Kaar said, "They just laid all the contracts face down and picked ours. Luck of the draw."

The Kaars, from Stanhope, New Jersey, had gone to a county fair where, Joan recalls, Rotonda boxes were everywhere, offering them a chance to "Win a Trip to Florida." She stuffed every box she could find and they won a trip to Miami—where she and her husband, a carpenter hoping for work in a growing community, were exposed to the Rotonda *Vision*.

When they came down later and saw Rotonda for real, they were disappointed. "There was nothing to see on the ground," Joan said. "But then they flew us over it. We could see the circle all laid out for roads and canals." Many of the early residents found Rotonda the same way.

Wesley and Lorraine Olson, from Montpelier, Vermont, won a trip to Palm Beach at the state fair at Rutland, Vermont.

"We were entertained by the Cavanagh people," Olson said. "I wasn't ready to retire but we bought some lots." That was in September 1970. Then they came down in October 1971 and stayed at the Holiday Inn in

Venice for a while, then became the thirteenth family to move in, on Rotonda Circle.

"An unlucky number, but it's been lucky for us," Olson said.

Rotonda pioneers Rosemary and Charles Toops attended a champagne party in their hometown, Cleveland, Ohio, and listened to Ed McMahon, Johnny Carson's jocular sidekick, pitching Rotonda to prospects.

Like hundreds of Rotonda buyers, the Toops bought their lot sight-unseen, with the understanding they could later get a refund or swap the lot. Eventually they swapped for their present lot in Oakland Hills on Golfview Court.

6.1 Pitchman Ed McMahon is shown plugging one of the early contests that built nationwide interest in Rotonda.

And so the community was born, a few homes scattered among mere traces on the ground of what Rotonda promised to become.

Among the early 1970s residents, besides the Kaars, Dodds, Olsons and Saunders, were Ron and Nancy Keebler, Ashley and Marge Beams, Frank and Fran Yust, Silvio and Ethel Furia, Billy and Lorena Phillips, and Arthur and Marion Shields. Also, among others, George and Millie Cheney, Larry and Marjorie Van Nattan, Joe and Marie Spezzano, Fred and Kathryn Parmelee, Vince and Marion Martino, and George and Neetia Herring.

The Kaars, Olsons, Toops and the Furias are still here, but the others are now only names to remember as the nucleus of the fledgling community.

While the new residents struggled to become acclimatized, Cavanagh worked its sales network hard, paying lavish up-front commissions. Prominent local attorney Guy Batsel remembers the salesmen having "cases of liquor and piles of blank sales contracts in their car trunks."

Joe Obey, a Michigander who would later become president of the Rotonda West Property Owners Association, remembers chatting with a Cavanagh salesman who eventually earned $140,000 in commissions in one year. "It was February," Obey said, "and already he had made over $50,000."

Obey found Rotonda from a sign on U.S. 41 near Venice in 1971, while driving by. "They had five model homes and the golf course, that was about all," Obey said. "I think I remembered seeing Rotonda mentioned in a golf magazine." Obey bought a lot on Oakland Hills Court, built his home in 1976, and retired and moved in a year later.

Besides their aggressive selling, Cavanagh worked the media to put Rotonda on the map.

- The *Miami Herald*, August 24, 1969: "Cavanagh Leasing Corp. has acquired 25,000 acres on Florida's west coast . . . says development will begin in near future."
- The *Sarasota Journal*, July 29, 1969: " 'Rotonda living seen at Cape Haze . . . not a retirement town nor a leisure world,' Klein says."
- The *Stuart News*, September 21, 1969: "Cavanagh Leasing plans to develop a new corporation to build Rotonda project in Charlotte County."
- The *Miami Beach Reporter*, August 31, 1969: " 'We are most enthusiastic about the acquisition of this ideally located acreage,' Mr. Klein said."
- The *St. Petersburg Times*, August 27, 1969: "The Rotonda concept, as explained to county officials last month, is an all-electric city-in-the-round."

- The *Tampa Tribune*, September 14, 1969: "A complete city is planned."

The *Fort Myers News-Press*, September 17, 1969, quoted Charlotte County officials who had three years earlier predicted, " the large undeveloped area at Cape Haze will one day be a new city rivaling St. Petersburg."

The media portrayed Charlotte County officialdom as euphoric about Rotonda's arrival. At the time, county politicos were loudly projecting that the county's 34,000 population would swell, in short order, to 95,000, completely altering its makeup.

Sure enough, all over the United States, in Canada and Europe, Rotonda lots were selling like hotcakes. The dismal failure of Rotonda East was either ignored or forgotten in the glow of Rotonda West's early success.

Meanwhile, inside Rotonda work was under way on the new $500,000 sewer collection and water system to serve the first subdivision, Oakland Hills.

And homes were being started. "We hope to have the first homes under construction, in blocks of thirty to forty, within the next thirty days," Cape Cave executive Jim Petrides said with rather extreme optimism. This would bring the project to Christmas 1970, and 150 families would be living in Oakland Hills by Spring 1971 — if he were right.

He wasn't. First residents Harry and Joan Kaar actually moved into their home in October 1971.

Cavanagh barged ahead, however, oblivious to minor irritants brought to them by early residents who felt their complaints were being ignored. While homes were not being completed as promised, the company was overlooking no aspect of sales. They built "in record time" a modular Rotonda sales office on the east side of State Road 775.

Built by Rotonda Development Corporation (RDC), the building had redwood siding and cedar shake shingles and a verandah with wide glass expanses.

Perhaps significantly, Stan Baumann, who headed RDC, noted that the structure was almost completed while its architectural plans were still being drawn. The company's inclination to work around or ahead of sound architectural planning would become evident later to residents.

The new sales building quickly became active. It housed eight offices, a kitchen, and a hospitality room. The massive $40,000 theater-in-the-round scale model was brought over from Palm Beach—the same unit banished by East Coast authorities for presenting a misleading portrayal of the eventual community.

Interest in Rotonda was nationwide. Marcus Gleisser wrote in The *Cleveland Plain Dealer* (September 1970) about the "grand opening of the unusual new development adjacent to Cape Haze . . . a community the company calls its city of the future."

According to Gleisser, a Cavanagh sales agency in Cleveland, Universal Properties, Inc., took a planeload of Ohioans to Rotonda to show off "the newest in city design . . . a community-in-the-round, with its future commercial core: office buildings, shopping, high-rise apartments."

During the Grand Opening, September 1970, a Cape Cave official was quoted, boasting: "We've taken deposits for twenty-one homes and lots." He added that, while a public turnout of 500 to 2,000 was expected, "actually 12,000 came . . . suggesting the interested must have wanted to visit Rotonda badly, because it's not just around the corner."

Dorothy Saunders Cannon remembers the opening. "More people came to Rotonda on opening day than went to the opening of Disney World."

The attraction that day, mused the Punta Gorda *Daily Herald-News*, "may have been the free hot dogs, or the chance to see Ed McMahon." Indeed, Dorothy said she and her late first husband, Mike Saunders, came to the grand opening just to see Ed McMahon. They saw him. As a result, they wound up buying a house and were first to sign a Rotonda sales contract.

McMahon figured prominently in the promotional hype surrounding Rotonda West's early days. Cavanagh's Klein had publicly claimed that McMahon was "a substantial investor in Rotonda West property, who will have a home here and be an active officer of the company." Sure enough, McMahon was much in evidence, greeting people during the grand opening and darting around the site being photographed the way celebrities do.

Delivery of the homes sold during the opening was promised for February 1971 (eight full months before the Kaars finally got to move in). By the fall of 1970, seven model homes, fully furnished and each with a pool, had been built on Golfview Terrace. The homes were priced, excluding lot, from $22,100 to $36,300. They were all ranch or split-level variations of the models.

They were built by Cavanagh's in-house construction arm. In an interesting community-relations move, Cape Cave denied access to the area's independent builders, "to protect the integrity and quality of building at Rotonda," according to a corporate bulletin. This brought a frustrated chuckle from early buyers still waiting for their homes to be ready.

This policy—Rotonda's builders constructing all homes—would remain in effect until June 1974 after 315 homes had been completed and another 208 were at various stages.

Some of these were of dubious quality as it turned out, although a Cavanagh official was quoted in the *Daily Herald-News* in January of 1974, "when we reached a certain level and set the tone for the houses we wanted, we always intended to invite other quality builders."

Even this policy shift, when it took place in 1974, proved profitable as Cavanagh required outside builders to pay them a percentage of the house price for the "privilege" of building in Rotonda. "I think it was 13 percent," said Joe Obey.

By that time most residents thought the policy change was a good idea. Unfortunately it was too late for some of the early arrivals who had substantial problems with their houses.

The Art of Building

THE CONTRACTOR was on the phone to Joe Obey. "Your garage is on the right side," the contractor said.

"Wrong," said Obey. The garage was supposed to be on the left, Obey said, but the contractor told him the slab was already poured and "it set up real pretty."

"I told him he'd have to flip the slab," Obey said, "but he said he couldn't do that, so I told him he had a problem."

Obey's story, plus those of many others, suggests ragtag building crews with questionable talents and lax supervision.

Obey remembers meeting Cavanagh's security chief, a former bodyguard for Chicago Mayor Richard Daley. The man had won $25,000 at craps in Las Vegas and immediately put his winnings down on a Rotonda house through a sales agent hovering nearby.

"The guy came here and got a job in security with Cavanagh," Obey said. "The first thing he did was run a check on all Cavanagh transient construction-site employees, turning up murderers, rapists, thieves and other felons by the dozen."

Obey remembers an enormous amount of theft in these early days. "As fast as appliances were put in houses they were stolen," he said. "They'd turn up in flea market sales."

First resident Joan Kaar was equally blunt, saying "they just didn't know what they were doing."

The Kaars had wanted to build their own home. "They wouldn't let us," Joan Kaar said. "We wound up doing everything over the phone — choosing colors for the floors, paneling, and other things we wanted."

Then the Kaars came down in July 1971 because their house was supposed to be ready. It wasn't. They had to rent a place to live until October. The developer paid only one month of their rent.

"We were mad, disgusted," Joan said. "They kept stalling because things weren't hooked up. Then we found the work on it was so sloppy . . . the walls had no framing behind. We made them rip it out and put in proper studding."

Harry Kaar said he had the title searched before they finally moved in. "There was a labor lien against it," he said. "Cavanagh hadn't paid one of the tile contractors."

The Kaars also felt like pioneers their first months in residence. "People would mistake our house for a model," Joan said. "We'd come home and find people going through it, so we started locking it. Then people would walk around and look in the windows, so we had to pull the shades."

Rosemary Toops remembers going around saying, "You can't do it that way," and "You've gotta be kidding," as the Rotonda building crews worked on changes she wanted. "Their level of competence was very low," Toops said. "The inside woodwork was poorly finished. You'd get splinters if you ran your hand down it."

She also remembers the construction crew bringing in a semi-trailer of cement. "The guys dumped the sacks off the truck, they all split and dust flew everywhere."

Helen Waldron, for years Rotonda's pre-eminent woman golfer, had lived first in Cape Haze, then moved to Cape Haze East. Waldron said, of many early residents, "They were told their houses were ready, but when they came down the houses weren't ready."

Waldron said she knew the man who headed sales for Cavanagh. "He told us it didn't matter how they sold it, so long as they sold it," she said. "They'd take prospects through Cape Haze, claim a house there belonged to Mr. White, president of White Sewing Machine Company. None of that was true."

As to the competence level of the building crews, Waldron agrees with others. "They had a labor problem. They had to literally drag workers in off the streets. Some of them were downright incompetent."

George and Yolanda Manyak came from Norwalk, Ohio, where George ran a successful Ford dealership. George bought his property in early 1972 without Yolanda seeing it. It was on Oakland Hills Court, overlooking the fourth tee of The Sunday Course (The Hills).

"They probably figured we'd get disgusted and quit, because it took eighteen months to build," Manyak said. "But in the auto business you learn to protect yourself. I'd set it up that if they didn't complete it in 120 days, they'd pay my rent until it was finished." The Manyaks lived rent free for fourteen of the eighteen months they waited, moving in, finally, in 1973.

Francis Labar—Jack to friends and to customers of his Lemon Bay Hardware store and Labar's pool service—bought several Rotonda lots as an investment in 1970.

"It was craziness," Labar says. "We kept getting things in the mail, they were pouring the slab, then putting up the walls. But when I came down, finally, to see how it was doing, it wasn't. It never was built."

The developer then reneged on an agreement that the Labars could trade the lots they owned for a single lot. They had to get an attorney to get everything straightened out. Finally, in disgust, they bought a house already completed. Labar would later become a president of the Rotonda West Property Owners Association.

Ed and June Melton came to Florida from Northbrook, Illinois in October 1972. Their house, the fifty-seventh in Rotonda West and promised to be ready for occupancy, was still under construction. The Meltons had to find temporary quarters, at Brook-To-Bay in Englewood, while their home was being finished.

June Melton visited the house one day while workers were putting in a bathroom. "They installed the toilet right in the doorway from the patio," June said. "When I complained, the guy said it was fine, 'low enough to step over.' When we took the matter to the office, they simply said, that's the way the plans are."

Disheartened, June went off to the beach leaving her irate husband Ed to work things out. Ed Melton hauled someone down to see the mispositioned toilet. "When he opened the door and saw the thing square in the doorway, he said, 'Oh my god,' " said Melton. "It turned out there were thirty-nine models, not yet built, where the plans were identical, the toilet in the doorway."

Joe Tringali also has his horror story. But in messing with Tringali, Cavanagh miscalculated. Tringali was a career army man who retired with the rank of colonel after thirty-five years of service in various parts of the world. He and his wife, Inge, had never owned a home, so their Rotonda home would be that much more precious to them.

When Tringali was informed that his house was ready he arranged for the military to ship his furniture, while he drove down. "I went looking for my house, 258 Caddy Road," Tringali said. "No house. Caddy Road wasn't even built yet. I thought I must be mixed up."

He wasn't of course, Cavanagh was. At the office, Tringali asked where the house was—the house in the progress photos they'd sent him—and was told, "There must be a mistake. But don't worry, we'll build you a house."

7.1 Col. Joseph A. Tringali, (ret.) turned out to be a major force in the development of Rotonda, as first president of the Property Owners Association, then as three-term Charlotte County Commissioner. (Courtesy of J. A. Tringali)

So, as many others were forced to do in these early days, the Tringalis had to store their furniture and rent a place to live. They began in a bedroom in a converted barn on Ainger Creek, and moved later to a condo on Englewood Beach Road.

"They were going to take care of it," Tringali said. "But they never did."

Resigned to it all, Tringali golfed while his house was being built. He played frequently with the first Rotonda golf pro, Walter ("Red") Lathrup, because "there was nobody else to play with."

One day, while on the seventeenth tee, Tringali looked across to see how work on his house was progressing. "They were just putting the roof on," he said, "and I could see the whole thing was slanted, not level. So, I walked over and pointed this out, but the guy in charge couldn't see anything wrong with it."

Tringali proceeded to show the man, using a tape measure, that the roof was one foot higher at one end than the other. It turned out the crew chief didn't know how to properly use a surveyor's transit. Tringali had to show him.

But Tringali's problems were far from over. He then noticed that his roof wasn't fastened to the walls. When he asked what was supposed to hold it down, he was told that the weight of the roof with its tile would be adequate. (The county's building code required it to be tied down)

Which recalls a comment by one irate resident, who requested anonymity due to on-going litigation, "I was a building inspector up north . . . and when I saw the way they were building here at Rotonda, I had visions of roofs flying all over the county if there was a tropical storm."

Tringali eventually forced the construction chief to anchor his roof with hurricane straps.

"So, I retired from the army in February 1972," Tringali said. "In March we came down to move into a house supposedly ready for us — remember they'd even sent us pictures — and we finally got into it in September." The Tringalis rented living quarters at their own expense for almost six months.

Cavanagh had plenty of reason to regret having jerked Joe Tringali around. Once he got his feet on the ground in Rotonda, Tringali was the prime mover in founding the Rotonda West Property Owners Association, the organization which would look out for the interests of the property owners. The POA would give Cavanagh fits during the ten years it owned Rotonda.

Englewood resident Larry Nicol agrees that some of the early building work was shoddy, even where it compied with building code. Nicol was in charge of Cavanagh's initial building program, running a crew of one hundred fifty men with five foremen, but would leave after less than a year, thoroughly dissatisfied with Cavanagh's "way of working."

Before he left, however, Nicol had supervised construction of the original seven model homes and then about one hundred thirty others for residents. "Things were going crazy then," he said. Nicol referred to his Cavanagh bosses as "a bunch of five-hundred-dollar-suit guys. I didn't trust any of them, except for Mr. P."

Mr. P., it turned out, was Jim Petrides, "A great guy," according to Nicol, who had his hands full more with head office interference than with his building job.

Nicol said, "I'd fire a sub-contractor—maybe he was double charging us, or doing shoddy work. Whatever, the head office often directed that subs I'd fired be re-hired. You figure why. We also had a retired architect, Norman Coates, to do inspections. He was pretty good, but Cavanagh fired him."

Nicol recalls starting the Kaar's house and then being pulled off it onto some other project by the sales office. This may explain why the Kaars, and others, had to seek temporary shelter until their houses were ready.

"There was a panic once," Nicol recalls. "I was told Ed McMahon was coming down to check the progress on his house, and we hadn't even started it yet. I had to get fifteen volunteers at time-and-a-half to lay the thing out in a hurry over a weekend, then look like they were working on it when McMahon showed up.

"Then, here came a fleet of Cadillac limos, McMahon and the five-hundred-dollar-suit guys and a camera crew. It was almost a hundred degrees that day. McMahon walked around, then offered to buy beer for the crew. One of the guys was dispatched with a twenty to get the beer and comes back with a case of Schlitz," Nicol laughed. "The five-hundred-dollar suits were horrified, knowing that McMahon huckstered Budweiser, and here were all these cameras recording everything."

As for the free swimming pool, television and carpeting that Cavanagh offered in the first one hundred homes, Nicol said, Cavanagh tried to make him eat that cost, about $5,000 per house.

"They just wanted to break even," Nicol said, "while I was trying to get a modest 8½ percent profit." So Nicol quit.

Later, with considerable fanfare, Edward J. Gerrits, Jr., agreed, "in a multi-million-dollar arrangement" to quote a *Rotonda Bulletin*, to manage Rotonda Development Corporation and direct all construction. The Gerrits firm was hailed as a major builder, with offices in St. Croix, Virgin Islands, and Puerto Rico.

The agreement would cover three years during which $105 million in building was projected, at a completion rate of four to eight units per day, according to Cavanagh.

Interestingly enough, despite the initial problems many residents had with their homes, most have stayed on at Rotonda.

"We have no regrets," said Joe Obey. "If this place had folded leaving just Oakland Hills, we'd still be ahead of the game."

Said Ed Melton, "We love it here. We wouldn't live anywhere else. The local people in Englewood, the stores and banks, were just great helping us move in."

Wesley Olson: "We were disappointed that the vision originally presented didn't come out that way. They painted a very rosy picture but much of it never materialized. But we love it here. We've been happy, made lots of friends."

George Manyak: "There aren't many places with this weather where you can go in, get a lot, build a house, full water and sewer connected, three golf courses, the Gulf nearby, all for such a nominal amount of money."

And Bob Antes: "The basic concept was super. This is one of the finest communities in Florida . . . quiet . . . limited access . . . secure. We've never been sorry that we came to Rotonda."

Meanwhile, remember the names Tringali and Antes. Both would figure prominently as Rotonda developed into a full-fledged community.

The Early Years

BY MID-1972 Cavanagh Communities Corporation was trumpeting the success of its Rotonda project.

The company's 1971 annual report said that a lush new golf course had opened for play a year ahead of schedule. "Described by visiting professionals as one of the best in Florida," the report said it was the first of seven planned courses.

Around the site of Oakland Hills the noise of jack-hammers, drills and earth movers filled the air as six hundred workmen went about their business.

The Cavanagh sales machine, operating from a network of forty-six sales offices across the U.S. and one in Geneva, Switzerland, was producing results. An economic study issued by the developer claimed that as of September 15, 1971, 15,113 platted lots had been sold from an inventory of 22,900. Also, they said, 2,781 multi-unit residential lots had been sold from 3,491 available.

As of December 31, 23,680 feet of sewer mains and 24,220 feet of water pipe had been laid. A tertiary sewage treatment plant had been built to provide purified sewer water to irrigate the golf course, and a reverse osmosis water treatment plant for the production of potable water had been dedicated.

The Rotonda airport landing strip had been lengthened to 4,200 feet to accommodate modern private aircraft.

The company claimed that 7,820 feet of "navigable" freshwater canals had been dug, 19,000 feet of electric and telephone cable had been installed, and more than 20,000 feet of paved road had been completed.

In addition, 5,366 single-family homes had been contracted for and home construction was active, with thirty homes per month being "delivered." The first condominium complex, Riverhouse, was well along with seventy-two units ready for tenants and the first 136 units presold.

Bill Futterer, working with a later developer management company, found some of the early sales statistics "mind-boggling." He said, "I read that they were selling lots at a rate of eight hundred a month," and noted that in 1993 all the builders in Charlotte County would build only about 1,300 homes. "The biggest year in county building history saw only twenty-five hundred [single family] homes built," Futterer said.

There is, of course, a difference between selling lots and building homes. Real estate experts in the early 1970s believed that, in a community like Rotonda, lot sales should not exceed home sales by more than 3:1. Only thus would property values be maintained. Cavanagh's own reports indicated a ratio of lots to homes sold at more than 20:1, suggesting that lot sales were far ahead of the development of supportive community amenities and infrastructure.

Many feel these numbers should have red-flagged trouble ahead. With lot prices ranging from $4,500 to $6,000, many of which were being financed by Cavanagh at 7½ percent, the company was generating huge amounts of cash. A substantial percentage of this should have gone into more and faster development of the community, early residents said, but it didn't. In Wesley Olson's opinion, "They were out to get as many bucks as they could, for their own purposes."

Certainly the numbers being floated were huge. In 1972, Cavanagh claimed a retail value exceeding $200 million for its unsold property on the Cape Haze peninsula, based on prevailing prices.

Cavanagh was now being viewed as rich and successful. *The Vision* was being energetically touted. This would be a dream community, with seven golf courses and marinas, a modern commercial center, canals and waterways galore—even a revolving restaurant at the hub, from which Rotonda's own private island beach would be visible.

Many early buyers heard only the appealing verbal sales pitch, saw only brochures the color of liquid sunshine selling them a vision beyond reality. They didn't read the small print.

Joe Klein kept a step ahead of everyone. Fully aware of Cavanagh's growing reputation as "a lot-selling machine," he outlined, in the company's 1971 annual report, "a dramatic change in the character of the company."

Henceforth, Klein declared, while Cavanagh would continue its role as a major homesite marketing company, emphasis had shifted toward construction and community development. He said that such a change was merely sound business judgment, noting, "the homesite sales and development business is capital intensive."

The corporation obviously was looking to improve its cash flow and strengthen its overall financial position, which was tenuous during most of 1971 due to a serious shortage of working capital.

Cavanagh reported net earnings in 1971 of $8 million on sales of over $53 million, a 25 percent earnings decline from 1970. However, a public offering brought in $9 million, the float was increased, and $25 million in financing was arranged through a consortium of banks and Ford Motor Credit Company. This was based mostly on Rotonda's potential.

In the two years since Cavanagh had acquired the land from the Vanderbilts the company had sold over three thousand acres for more than $70 million, with another three thousand acres allocated to public use, according to the annual report.

Klein was talking now about a marketing technique he called "controlled growth." Selected residential lots would be withheld from the market for later sales under building compulsion contracts. This policy required that lot buyers henceforth had to build within a year, and was intended to maintain resale values and balance supply and demand.

Said Klein, "In 1972 we expect decreased financing costs, increased monthly payment collections and increased cash profits from home construction."

Cavanagh also was one of the first major developers to assess lot owners for improvements—water and sewer facilities, $1,200 for a single family lot, $1,200 plus another $225 per unit for multi-family units. These charges had to be paid in twenty equal semi-annual payments beginning two years from the signing of the sales agreement. As they began construction, lot owners would be charged additional for water and sewer hookup—$200 for water and $225 for sewer.

While the early residents hoped their community would develop as *The Vision* projected it, there were hardheaded skeptics.

Charles Toops didn't believe the community would support seven golf courses and seven marinas by the specified date, December 31, 1977. "To support all these golf courses and restaurants and stores in Center City [the commercial area in the hub] didn't make economic sense," he said, adding, "we didn't always believe all we heard about Rotonda." Jack Labar thought that in the long run things might have worked out for Cavanagh, "but they were never going to do it in the five years they were predicting. Any reasonable businessman could see that it just wasn't going to happen," Labar said. However, Cavanagh plowed on.

8.1 This 1971 photo shows the development just beginning to get under way. The Oakland Hills subdivision is to the upper left.

Work was under way outside the circle by now:
• The Lakes, a 1,127 acre subdivision, was 47 percent sold.
• The Heights was 74 percent sold. "It overlooks Buck Creek which flows into the Intracoastal waterway," a Cavanagh booklet said, inferring Gulf access. Its 827 acres included a strip set aside for marine-oriented businesses, and was being developed to be "a center for every type of water sports, including sailing, water skiing and fishing."

- Rotonda Sands was 43 percent sold; its 2,626 acres "crisscrossed by an intricate system of navigable canals."
- Rotonda Shores was 405 acres "that should appeal to water sports enthusiasts . . . it faces the West Branch of Coral Creek, a 1,000-foot-wide channel that flows into the Intracoastal Waterway," another inference of Gulf access. Sales in The Shores were about to begin.
- Rotonda Meadows acreage also was not yet sold, but was about to go on the market. This was a 1,100-acre subdivision "with a natural creek whose waters will be used to create two fresh-water lakes."

One can argue the extent to which Cavanagh's sales brochures and documents implied direct water access to the Gulf of Mexico. Many argue that they did. Many more said the salesmen, in their verbal pitches, made no bones about it.

According to Ed Melton, "Look at their original brochures. They say they're on the Gulf of Mexico. In other words your boat can get from Rotonda's canals . . . or from the marinas that never happened . . . into the Intracoastal and then the Gulf itself."

Bill Hyde sees the issue of Gulf access as an early indication of future problems. Hyde, now executive vice-president of Englewood Bank and a teen-ager in early Rotonda, said, "I think the first real controversy concerned the belief that Rotonda was supposed to be linked with Buck Creek, and thus, through the canal system, would access the Gulf for their boats."

That controversy, however, would explode later.

While Cavanagh's sales tactics were aggressive, this was a time when Florida real estate sales functioned in the context and spirit of "Buyer Beware."

However, attorney Guy Batsel of Batsel, McKinley, Ittersagen and Gunderson said, "I spent three months negotiating a contract with Joe Klein in Miami. We walked in having heard all these horror stories about him being a crook. We walked out thinking just the opposite."

Said Batsel, "It's unfair to judge a man . . . let me put it this way, the ethics of real estate marketing in the late sixties were entirely different than they are now."

Batsel pointed out that Cavanagh was doing what everyone else in that business was doing. "That doesn't make it right," he conceded, "but until just a few years ago, 'Buyer Beware' was the unwritten law in

Florida land sales and real estate." The lawyer noted that Cavanagh's tactics were not unusual, and had been, in fact, successfully defended in the courts. "The courts allowed it to happen," he said.

In this, Batsel is correct. In a later class action, one of the few to actually go to trial in Charlotte County Circuit Court, a jury found Cavanagh and its Cape Cave subsidiary "not guilty" of fraud and misrepresentation in its sale of lots.

8.2 Aerial view of the Oakland Hills subdivision showing the "space ship" and first Rotonda homes, circa 1972. The layout of the Sunday golf course (The Hills) can be seen. (Photo courtesy Cape Haze Realty Co.)

To this day questions are raised about Cavanagh's intent for Rotonda. Was the company serious about *The Vision* they were pitching so aggressively—seven golf courses, marinas, navigable canals, a commercial hub, tower restaurant and all—or was that all the syrup to sell the pancakes?

The syrup was certainly obvious. A typical brochure talked about it all, in glittering prose, right down to: " . . . you'll enter Rotonda West through one of four guarded entrances." But at the bottom, in small type, the legal qualifier was evident: "Purchaser should not rely on any fixed time for development or completion. . . . "

The plan was certainly do-able, experts believe, under certain conditions that are obvious in hindsight. One of these conditions was solid and consistent financing, and another was a reasonable cash flow.

When the economy "went South" in the early 1970s interest rates soared to 21.5 percent, making money for infrastructure development hard to borrow. Treatment of passive income by the new tax structure impacted the condo business in Florida, which virtually died as a result. The tax reform act of 1986 then eliminated deductions for some vacation homes, so the dream of "A Winter Home in Florida" became harder for many to realize.

These realities hurt Cavanagh at a time when Rotonda was just getting off the ground.

However, the developer may also have shot itself in the foot by mismanaging what they had. They needed sound management working a workable plan, particularly one that narrowed the ratio between lot and home sales. The early residents also claim "the developer didn't foster a good relationship with us . . . prefers to react to confrontational approaches." And there were plenty of these.

"After all," said one resident, "if they'd simply acknowledged our existence we'd have helped them sell Rotonda by bragging about it."

John Lawson, a former police officer from New York, said, "Everyone here was at odds with Cavanagh, and they with us. They'd send spies into our meetings in the Community Center. The whole atmosphere was hostile."

Another critical point, according to Bill Futterer, "Cavanagh had poor relations with most state and county agencies." He noted that, in a development of this size, "you have to work closely with state agencies, the Departments of Natural Resources, Environmental Protection, Community Affairs, and especially the Florida Division of Land Sales."

This was certainly true in one area that Cavanagh might not have predicted, but which drastically altered their plans: the environment.

When the original plans for Rotonda East were germinating, "ecology" was a word few understood. In the early 1960s, environmentalists were regarded as "long-haired tree-huggers and bunny-lovers." Who could have predicted that government in the early 1970s would spew forth a rash of federal, state and local laws, regulations and agencies mandated to protect mangroves, sea grass, gopher tortoises, eagles nests and scrub jays?

Passage of wetlands legislation stopping dredge-and-fill-type developments forced Cavanagh to make massive changes from what they had planned in 1969. Suddenly, large parts of their Rotonda acreage became undevelopable due to environmental considerations. This was particularly true of The Springs, which borders Charlotte Harbor, The Villas and Sands, St. Andrews, which straddles Coral Creek, and Don Pedro Island.

Even in the early 1990s, Rotonda developers were in constant discussions with regulatory authorities about scrub jay protection in Windward. "In 1969," said Bill Futterer, "nobody thought about scrub jays." Futterer emphasized the immediate problem these new environmental concerns created—the thousands of lots already sold, which now could not be developed as promised.

8.3 Early view of Oakland Hills looking toward the Gulf of Mexico over Don Pedro Island showing development in the hub and the beginnings of Pebble Beach golf course on the right.

Finally, again, the matter of Gulf access. Whether or not it ever would have been feasible, the question of Gulf access from Rotonda's canals was firmly settled—it never would happen. Environmentalists blanched at the very idea of mixing fresh and salt water just to permit passage for boats.

To his credit, by 1971 Joe Klein was not unaware of the impact of environmental matters on his development of Rotonda West. He'd already clashed with authorities in Palm Beach and Martin counties on such matters as they applied to Rotonda East before he transferred his vision to the Cape Haze peninsula.

In the company's 1971 annual report, Klein wrote "Cavanagh's planning . . . has shown an unswerving determination to preserve the peninsula's natural environment."

Early residents, exposed as they were to a landscape made barren to facilitate construction—with billowing clouds of sand one of the results—chuckled derisively at Klein's claim that "homes are being built with meticulous concern for the preservation of natural foliage." A $240 million state bond issue passed in 1972 included funds for aquisition of environmentally sensitive lands bordering the Cape Haze peninsula.

Environmental issues were not Cavanagh's only concern, however. The Arabs, who provided 60 percent of America's oil, suddenly embargoed oil shipments to the U.S. in an attempt to force the U.S. government to pressure Israel to make concessions in Middle East negotiations.

The ensuing oil crisis, and the subsequent home building and real estate recession of the early 1970s, added another burden to the developer's operations.

"That's when things started unraveling," Bill Futterer said. "The economy went sour. People stopped buying gas and traveling. All this crunched Cavanagh, who, we assume, was highly leveraged at the time."

Go back to the question many ask, did Cavanagh really intend to develop Rotonda as *The Vision* outlined it? Though most doubt it, one piece of evidence supports the contention that they might have.

This was a twenty-six-page booklet that Cavanagh used internally titled: "The Commercial Generating Principle (CGP) . . . Key to Rotonda's Planned Growth." It was dated December 20, 1972.

It began with a definition of Rotonda. This would be not just a residential community, not just a play-resort, not just a city providing commercial opportunities—but a combination of all three. The CGP purported to be the result of an economic study of the long-range development of Rotonda, on which the building schedule was based.

Joe Klein began the CGP by noting sales to date of over 15,000 separate Rotonda lots for more than $100 million.

The theory Klein then expounded was that completion of each aspect of Rotonda's development would stimulate further growth. Building homes creates jobs, for example. These in turn provide income, which stimulates consumer demand. This generates the need for shops, stores, restaurants and other commercial facilities, which create more jobs which increase the need for more housing.

A sort of circle of perpetual growth, this was presented as if the Holy Grail had been discovered, even though it was well known and fundamental logic.

But the CGP also outlined "Minimum Goals for Rotonda Growth through 1977." Population, for example, would go from twenty-five hundred in mid-1973 to thirty thousand by December of 1977.

The commercial, professional, service and related facilities—and financial requirements—to support this growth were spelled out in twenty pages of charts and graphs. On page nine, for example, it stated that a population of five hundred would support a post office, a liquor store, a service station, a convenience store and a drug store.

When the population reached nine thousand, according to the CGP, all sorts of new facilities would become feasible—an art store, boat dealers and storage yards, cabinet makers, a bakery, attorneys, medical and dental clinics, even an auto dealership.

This reflected Klein's idea of a self-contained community. One can assume the bulk of these businesses were to be in the Commercial Center in the hub.

In fact, for a time Rotonda had a restaurant, a small deli, a gas station, the postal sub-station, and, eventually, a bank. In time, most of the facilities the CGP listed did become available in the communities surrounding Rotonda outside the circle, suggesting the validity of the concept itself.

For example, Jack Labar started Lemon Bay Hardware and a pool service. In like manner, soon there was a boutique, an insurance agency and a pizza parlor, all businesses started and run by Rotonda residents.

The CGP went on to spell out the schedule of amenities construction: A recreational park on thirty acres in The Shores, for example, to be completed January 31, 1973. This would include a regulation Little League baseball field, a full-sized football field, a banked quarter-mile running track, a playground for children, tennis courts, a barbecue and picnic area, a lake with beach and bandstand, restrooms, and locker facilities.

It all came to pass, though on a scale less grandiose than it was outlined. Certainly there was no beach or bandstand. But there would be a four thousand-square-foot community center completed by year-end 1972 on three lots on Cape Haze Drive with adjacent parking. It would include a working kitchen and could accommodate three hundred fifty people.

The CGP spelled out plans for the Oakland Hills clubhouse, beach and dock facilities on Don Pedro Island, and on Cape Haze Drive the strip shopping center, convenience store, service station (Texaco), and a small restaurant.

Those familiar with business plans know they require constant adjustment to changing economic and financial realities. Events obviously overtook Cavanagh, but there was a viable plan on paper, and in time most of it came to pass but not always when projected.

The clubhouse, for example, scheduled to open in August 1973, finally opened in 1978. The Monday course, scheduled for mid-1973, actually opened in 1989 as Pebble Beach and, subsequently, The Palms.

Was Cavanagh serious about *The Vision* they were selling? The CGP is one argument in their favor.

Meanwhile, the infant community conceived in September 1969, and born when Harry and Joan Kaar moved into residence in October 1971, was taking its first tottering steps by October 1972, with one hundred families in residence, two hundred thirty homes under construction and seventy-five more homes about to be started.

Social Security

IMMEDIATELY UPON their arrival, the early Rotonda residents reached out to each other for support in their strange new environment. They took up a wide range of activities and began to organize Rotonda's social life.

The first Christmas, which was 1971, the Saunders invited the first seventeen residents for potluck dinner. Dorothy Saunders Cannon remembers that dinner as the inaugural social event. Within a year, the social scene expanded.

"We were all from somewhere else," Ethel Furia pointed out. "We were all new to each other and new to the area. It was natural that we came together."

Ethel and Silvio Furia had come from Babylon, Long Island, in 1972 with their son Joseph. They were the seventh family in Rotonda. "We'd been in the restaurant business," Ethel said, "and felt too young to retire." So Silvio became manager of Smitty's, a well-known restaurant in Venice. He later managed the Captain's Club on Englewood Beach, but quit when the club's owner, Steve Ruth, was arrested and the place had acquired the reputation as a drug base. It has since become B.G. Snappers under new owners.

Ethel Furia became Cape Cave's director of community relations almost immediately upon her arrival, then started the *Rotonda Bulletin*, which she typed, mimeographed, then delivered herself. "The post office didn't like that," Furia chuckled. "It wasn't stamped."

Cape Cave Corporation supported Furia's fledgling editorial effort and paid for its printing and distribution. They allowed her to run it, but they controlled the content, using the newsletter as their vehicle to communicate with the residents.

However, Ethel Furia's editorial efforts did help to mold the community by conveying personal information and social notes that kept everyone aware of new arrivals, organizations and meetings. The *Bulletin* would give way, in 1979, to the *Rotonda Review*, "to serve a growing community," and it began to accept advertising to defray expenses. Ed Melton would become the *Review*'s advertising salesman.

9.1 Ethel and Silvio Furia. Ethel has been the "town crier" ever since she and her husband became the seventh in residence. Even today she writes and edits the *Rotonda Review*.

By 1974 several social groups had been established and were in full swing. These included: The Fiesta Association, American Legion, U.S. Coast Guard Auxiliary, men and women's golf associations, the Round Town Garden Club, a bridge club, a Boy Scout troop and a nondenominational church group.

One of the first to organize was American Legion Post 113. It got off the ground early due to sponsorship by Cavanagh, who, for some strange reason, awarded all home buyers, whether they were eligible or not, free Legion membership. The Legion thus mushroomed quickly. Clayton Rhodes was the first post commander.

Jack Labar recalls, "If you bought a lot you got Legion membership from Cape Cave, so we initially had a Legion Post with five hundred members but no Legion hall. We met in the community center like every other group in Rotonda."

9.2   American Legion officers prepare for the groundbreaking for the Legion building. From left: Sam Snyder, Jack Labar, Al Roberts, Ed Quick, and Jim Graham. Labar and Graham would also serve as presidents of the Rotonda West Property Owners Association.

Labar said, "We eventually wiped the membership rolls clean, started again from scratch and built a real Legion. We started working on the building then too, and got the corporation to donate land, which they first did out on Boulevard West where the churches now are. But that wasn't big enough, so we wound up building where the old recreation center used to be, where the Legion is now."

The Fiesta Association started in late 1971, with potluck suppers at various homes as people sought each other out, initiated new friendships, and began Rotonda's social whirl.

"Fiesta started right in our living room," recalls Dorothy Saunders Cannon. We had such a happy group of people here then."

By September 1972, Fiesta became official, its purpose—to embrace newcomers and provide social activity and fellowship in this strange new environment.

"Fiesta was the social organization that brought people together," said Jack Labar. "It introduced new arrivals. Because everyone was in the same boat, from somewhere else, we turned to each other, and also welcomed newcomers." Labar would later serve on the Fiesta board.

In a nod to early Spanish influence, Fiesta called its leader the "Alcalde" while the directors were "Conquistadores." They sported regalia that reflected the Spanish connection, and the colorful outfits spiced up the association's social events. As Dorothy Saunders Cannon noted, "this was a very Spanish area from its history."

9.3 The late Mike Saunders in full regalia as first Alcalde of the Fiesta Association, with Dorothy Saunders. The Saunders were the first to sign a Rotonda West sales contract. (Courtesy Dorothy Saunders Cannon)

Mike Saunders, first signer of a Rotonda sales contract and first postmaster at the Rotonda post office sub-station was the first elected Alcalde. His Conquistadores included Wesley Olson, Ed Dodds, Silvio Furia, Willard Phillips, Larry Van Nattan, Harry Kaar, Vince Martino, Fred Parmalee and Frank Yost.

Mike Saunders, a jovial extrovert, became the catalyst for much of the early social mixing. According to Dorothy, it was his idea to start the Fiesta. Saunders was described as a personable man who radiated fun and was popular with everyone. Unhappily, he would pass away in 1974 at Venice Hospital. When Mike died the new community mourned the loss of its first active leader.

Dorothy, Mike's widow, eventually married Jim Cannon and moved to Manasota Beach Road in Englewood. In 1994, at eighty, she was still spry and active.

Joan Kaar remembers the Rotonda community's formative years. "There were twenty-one of us at the first Fiesta meeting," she said. "We met in each other's homes until the group got too big and we moved into the community center. We'd get together once a month and bring newcomers along to be introduced around."

9.4 Early Fiesta Association Conquistadores in full regalia. From left: (front) J. C. Herring, Alcalde Larry Van Nattan, first Alcalde Michael Saunders, and Fred Parmalee; (rear) Ed Dobbs, George Fillon, Walter Davis, Harry Hoar, Milo Hall, Wesley Olson, D. S. Bentley, Willard Phillips, and Silvio Furia.

One of Ethel Furia's early *Bulletins*, for September 1972, reported: "The monthly potluck supper was a great success . . . Ellen Kerswold provided her special Norwegian meatball recipe . . . more than one hundred residents attended . . . Alcalde Saunders welcomed twenty-two newcomers," an indication of the Fiesta Association's rapid early growth.

Reading back issues of the *Rotonda Bulletin* gives the impression that, despite the trauma many early residents experienced getting into their new homes, the social life of the community was both active and varied.

One issue reports "a caravan of cars . . . to the Beachcomber Motel in Miami Beach . . . for a weekend of racing, nightclubs, jai alai, gourmet dining."

In the second year, Alcalde Saunders and his Conquistadores, working with Captain Bill Massey of the *Roundabout* (Cavanagh's Don Pedro ferryboat), decorated the boat and entered it in Englewood's Pioneer Days Parade.

"The men were colorfully decked out in full Spanish regalia," wrote Furia, "and were awarded first place for their efforts." The Rotonda community was proud.

Of that event, Dorothy Saunders Cannon said, "We knew we also needed a 'Miss Rotonda West.' Sheree Olson was the only female teen, and she was pretty so she was elected. We got a bumper sticker and taped it across her chest . . . it was a riot. We had such fun."

Suggesting that resident/developer differences had not yet broken into open confrontation, Ethel Furia wrote, in late Spring 1973, "This has been another busy month . . . one highlight, a cocktail party at which residents and Cavanagh executives met socially and discussed the community's development."

By 1974 contract bridge was in full swing, organized by Peggy Pelletier. The group started with seven players—an awkward number for a bridge game—but soon there were enough women bridge enthusiasts for three tables of combat every Wednesday afternoon. Lorraine Olson became chairlady of the Oakland Hills Bridge Club.

Rotonda West Lions Club was launched July, 1973, with a dinner at the community center. The club claims to be the first service organization in Rotonda. Fred Parmalee was the first president. George Herring and George Fillon were vice-presidents, Larry Van Nattan was secretary, and Barney Schmidlin was treasurer.

The first meeting of the U.S. Coast Guard Auxiliary was held May 15, 1973, and was attended by thirty-six eager Rotonda boat owners. The organizing push to put Flotilla 89 on Charlotte Harbor waters came from Ken and Gen Donovan. A retired electrical engineer from the Tennessee Valley Authority out of Tupelo, Mississippi, Donovan was a veteran boating enthusiast. He was familiar with boat safety matters and the dangers to small boaters that are posed by storms.

Donovan was sworn in as first commander in August 1973 when the unit's charter was presented. More than one hundred Coast Guard and Auxiliary officials attended the ceremony, where fifty-five charter members were installed. Flotilla 89 thus became part of USCGA's

Eighth Division, which includes the area from Anna Maria Island to Boca Grande Pass. Gen Donovan would become commander in 1978.

The Rotonda Woman's Club started in October 1973 and was chartered as a member of the Florida Federation of Woman's Clubs on May 1, 1974, with forty-three members. The club's motto was "Working Today for a Beautiful Tomorrow," and its aim was "To Ever Widen the Circle."

Within a year the club had indeed widened its circle, swelling its ranks to eighty-seven. Helen Allison was the first president, and it was her suggestion that the Woman's Club should erect the flagpole in the traffic circle on Cape Haze Drive. The American flag flies there today.

In 1976 the club gained nationwide attention among active club women by winning a Community Service Award, one of just three clubs to do so from among four hundred fifty clubs.

The Rotonda West Woman's Club was always one of the community's most active social organizations, participating in many area events, sponsoring seminars on issues for women, supporting the annual Cardiac Capers golf tournament and the Don Pedro Arts and Crafts Fair, and the Hacienda Girl's Ranch in Melbourne, Florida. Rotonda's own library, in the Community Center, was initiated by the Woman's Club. It was dedicated in January 1977 and now has more than five hundred books available for loan.

The roster of Woman's Club presidents includes women who were active and concerned about the social and service aspects of community life at Rotonda. Besides Helen Allison, who started the club, they were: Clair Syupek, Billie Dodds, Lois Maglietto, Fran Rokisky, Mary Bird, Marion Strunz, Ruth Sissea, Muriel Landman, Earlene Hankins, Corinne Van Kleek and Barbara Reilly.

While the social and service aspects of their lives were important to them, Rotonda residents new to Florida marveled at the variety of flora they were now exposed to. A group gathered and formed The Round Town Garden Club, where they could learn how to nurture the region's fascinating horticulture.

Joan Kaar recalls that Cape Cave, in the early 1970s, operated a full-scale nursery in Windward, where they sold plants and trees at reasonable prices. The nursery, unhappily, didn't last long as a going enterprise.

The Garden Club, however, like the Woman's Club, became active almost at once, holding seminars, show-off fairs, demonstrations and contests. Said Rosemary Toops, "Florida is a tough place to learn to grow grass and plants, with its undernourished and sandy soil, so the garden club was very popular."

At one Garden Club meeting it was noted that Rotonda West was habitat to more than three hundred species of plants native to Florida. At another, G. C. Herring displayed one of his "amazing" two-pound tomatoes and told the club members how to prepare the soil and develop a successful vegetable garden. Herring's own garden was said to yield, in one season, more than one hundred fourteen cucumbers and one hundred twenty tomatoes, which Herring claimed had a seventy-five dollar value on a thirty-two dollar investment.

In May of 1975, supersalesman Ed McMahon was awarded honorary membership in the Round Town Garden Club. He once received the "Yard of The Month Award," though nobody could recall ever seeing McMahon in his yard, far less tilling his soil.

By 1976 the Round Town Garden Club was a formidable local force. Members were kept busy with contests for best potted plant, best miniature arrangement, best horticultural specimen, best artistic presentation. These awards were won that year, respectively, by Ruth Will, Virginia Stockwell, Irene Traband, Stella Larson and Ethel Pitts. All-around winner, with most blue ribbons that year, was Marjorie Beams.

This 1976 show presented one hundred twenty-five entries in the Community Center, which the members turned into a tropical garden for the event. More than two hundred viewers and participants attended the show, proving the club's popularity.

It would not be until several years later that The Elks Lodge was formed, at the suggestion of Ray LaGoy, Rotonda's popular head golf pro, who arrived in 1979.

Said John Meadows, "Ray was one of the guys who conceived the idea for the Lodge, and he was elected its first Exalted Ruler." The Lodge quarters were located where the old restaurant used to be, in the shopping strip on Cape Haze Drive opposite the Community Center. The Elks moved in 1993 to larger, free-standing quarters on Boulevard East, near County Road 771.

LaGoy, in fact, urged John Meadows to become the official organist for The Elks, which he did. "I don't consider myself a pro, and never played publicly," Meadows said modestly, "but I'm still the Lodge organist."

The Rotonda Elks Lodge quickly drew members from other area Lodges, particularly Englewood and Port Charlotte, two of the largest lodges in Florida. Today, the Rotonda Elks number some seven hundred members, sponsor a Boy Scout troop, and have adopted Rotonda Boulevard West to keep clean in the Adopt-A-Road program.

Meeting dates, news and social tidbits were carried weekly in Ethel Furia's *Bulletin* from the beginning, which served to keep people informed and active. In fact, Furia's by now voluminous files contain the true social history of Rotonda.

And so, despite (and frequently unaware of) problems swirling around the developer, the early residents created their own community through their own efforts. Indeed, even in the early seventies Rotonda was becoming a real community, not just a sedentary backwater of life for retirees. Many people worked—and there were even kids here!

School Daze

ROTONDA WAS NOT just a sedentary retirement community. In fact, its early social swirl was stimulated as much by children as by adults. Many of the residents moved with their children: the Kaars with Joseph, the Olsons with Sheree and Terri, the Furias with Joe. Other early residents with youngsters were the Meltons, Manyaks, Antes, Quints, Labars and many others.

William and Donnell Hyde came from Ridgeway, Pennsylvania, in 1971. They lived in Cape Haze for about six months while their house was being built at 48 Golfview Court. It was the sixth house built in Rotonda. Their son, Bill, is now an executive with Englewood Bank. At the time he was only seventeen and his sister, Jane, was nineteen. His father passed away in 1992, but the family still owns their original house but now leases it out.

Bill Hyde remembers that Rotonda had a number of "kids" in these early years. The youngest would attend Englewood Elementary School in Sarasota County, and Lemon Bay Junior High was nearby, but the nearest high school was Charlotte High in Punta Gorda—a distance of almost twenty miles.

"We'd go on the bus to high school," Hyde said. "It took about forty minutes. Eventually I got a car, and I'd take Sheree Olson. The Olsons moved in about the time we did."

Traffic was lighter in these days because Port Charlotte was still relatively undeveloped. Murdock was mostly open range with cattle, instead of being filled with malls, banks and government facilities as it is today. In fact Bill Hyde remembers that the only thing in Murdock then was the DeSoto Groves fruit stand and the post office on U.S. 41.

The Hyde family came to Rotonda through their daughter Jane's friendship with Troy Petrides, whose father, Jim Petrides, worked for the Vanderbilts in the 1960s. Jim Petrides later moved to Rotonda to work for Cape Cave Corporation.

Jane Hyde persuaded her parents that Rotonda was the place to be, so they moved here too.

"It was a big change for us kids," young Bill Hyde said, "and for all the young people who came here from elsewhere. We all got close pretty quickly as more and more arrived."

Wes Olson also remembers these days and that his daughter, Sheree, and Bill Hyde were the first Rotonda children to graduate from Charlotte High School.

"To get to school they had to take the road through the 'Metropolis' (the hub) to get to Rotonda Boulevard East," he said. "It was a sandy dirt road then and they frequently got stuck."

Olson's youngest daughter, Terri, rode her bike all the way to State Road 775 to catch the bus to Englewood Elementary.

In 1972, the Furias became the seventh residents to arrive, bringing their son, Joseph. Then came the Meltons in 1973 with their son, Scott. In fact, by 1974, when Lemon Bay was still just a junior high, its student body included Joe Furia, Mike Long, Jill Brost, Clay Horton, Andy Kolba, C.J. Kraft, Joe and Cindy Chirillo, Tony Roberts, and Leslie Mink—all kids from Rotonda.

When home-builder Ed Quint and his wife, Beverly, arrived they brought daughters, Karen and Suzy. The Manyaks have two sons and two daughters, one of whom was attending the University of South Florida. "That was 1972," said George Manyak. "When we came down, my oldest son still had one credit to get [for graduation] and he went to Charlotte High with Bill Hyde. They played golf together there." Manyak chuckles, thinking back. "They shot consistently in the low seventies but couldn't even make the golf squad when they went to USF, where they had Fuzzy Zoeller and other big name golfers at the time. But my youngest daughter was the first girl to make the all-boys golf team in Englewood."

An early *Bulletin* from Ethel Furia reports that in mid-1972 Bill Hyde and Joe Furia were burning up the local golf courses in Greater Sarasota Golf Association events. Hyde usually won in his age group, with Furia taking frequent seconds and thirds in his group.

Scott Melton, meanwhile, was being named top pitcher in the Englewood Little League, with a record of nine wins and three losses and 1.9 earned-run average.

Rotonda kids were active in the Florida Association Amateur Athletic Union and hardly a month went by without community bulletins braying their accomplishments: Leslie Mink second in sprints . . . firsts in several events by Joe Furia, Dan Shields, Tony de Jack, Wendy Ferro, Holly Manyak, and seconds by Carl and Eric Kellem, Chris Sinclair, Tony Walshaw, Glen Korswold and Debby Froemisch . . . enough in fact for the group to trek to athletic meets as far away as St. Petersburg, traveling on U.S. 41 because I-75 had not yet been constructed. Their exploits were followed keenly by the close-knit Rotonda community.

By 1974 several Rotonda youngsters were on Lemon Bay Junior High's basketball team.

There were even enough youngsters in Rotonda in the early seventies to begin a Teen Center. A Junior Fiesta Association organized twenty kids for table tennis, skittles, chess and ice cream in "the old A-frame."

This structure, on Coral Creek Drive, preceded the community center on Cape Haze Drive, and was proclaimed the Teen Center in June 1973. It was donated by Cape Cave and fixed up by the residents, who also donated the games. Activities were supervised by twelve sets of parents who volunteered Mondays, Wednesdays and Fridays from 6:00 until 10:00 P.M.

Throughout the seventies Rotonda kids did much to stimulate community pride and make it an active, vibrant place to live.

The growth of Rotonda during the 1970s convinced county officials of the crying need for additional schools. The existing school plant had become overcrowded, due in part to Rotonda's growth. They began to study the situation.

Later, 1981 would be a watershed year in the lives of many Rotonda youngsters. Seeing the combined school population in the area from three counties — Sarasota, Lee (Boca Grande) and Charlotte — the state stepped in and finally upgraded Lemon Bay to full high school status. In June 1981 the first graduation from Lemon Bay High included twenty Rotonda students.

Jack Labar said, "the biggest plus living in Rotonda was the school system. We had two kids with us then. My daughter graduated from

Charlotte High and is now an administrative nurse. My youngest son is a physicist for NASA. The school system here did them well."

There was tragedy, too, in the community. In June 1981, twins Grace and Greg Paradiso received scholarship awards as seniors in that first graduating class. Paradiso's scholarship noted "his outstanding attributes as a student." Greg was killed in an auto accident that September, just shy of his eighteenth birthday. Rotonda mourned the loss of one of their outstanding young people. His scholarship money went into the Greg Paradiso Memorial Scholarship Fund. This became part of Lemon Bay's scholarship program, which today runs at an annual level of some $1.5 million, illustrating the strength of the Rotonda area schools.

In February 1984, ground was broken for L. A. Ainger Junior High, named after a longtime school board member. The thirty-six-acre site was donated by Cavanagh's Cape Cave Corporation. The company promised to build a permanent access road via Rebel Court, Bonita Drive and Concord Road, with continuation to State Road 776 via Spinnaker Boulevard. The work carried an estimated cost of $51,000.

An interesting note is that Joe Tringali, by now on the Charlotte County Commission, owned the property over which the access road would be built.

"The chairman of the School Board, Mac Horton, called and said they needed my lot," Tringali recalls. "Hell, I didn't even know where it was. I'd bought it in 1975 for four hundred down and eighty-five a month and it was paid for."

Tringali had about $23,000 in the property, including $2,300 in assessments, and he sold it to the School Board for what he had in it.

Shortly after the transaction, the *Fort Myers News-Press* newspaper carried a headline: "Commissioner Makes $12,000 Profit on Property Sold to School Board."

"The reporter had seen a property transfer note," Tringali said. "He just checked the price against what the appraiser's office listed, and figured the difference was profit . . . and didn't even call me. He just ran with it."

"There were letters to the editor about political sleaze and so forth . . . so I had to show them all the papers to clear myself. They printed a retraction, a tiny one," Tringali said, somewhat miffed. "Actually, when I quoted them the price I'd paid, I forgot to include all the assessment money."

L. A. Ainger was built in two phases. The first included the administration building, cafeteria, a vocational facility, and classrooms, built at a cost of $2.25 million.

Phase two, begun in fall 1984, added a library, physical education and music facilities and more classrooms, costing another $3.1 million.

The new school opened in August 1984 with construction still under way, and with three hundred forty-two students, and was dedicated November 27, 1984.

Vineland Elementary School, for kindergarten through fifth grade, on Boundary Boulevard would follow in 1987.

"The developer sold the land for Vineland," Tringali said, although we had an oral agreement that land was dedicated to public use. They reneged. I was mad as hell [because the developer originally had promised to donate the land]."

The community, which started in 1971 with one family with one child, had its first on-site school in just thirteen years.

Faith Was Strong

S OCIAL ACTIVITY increased as more families took up residence. Now small groups of committed Christians were getting
together, determined to establish Rotonda's first churches. Sur-
veys had been done informally, suggesting thirty-seven Protestant, forty-
two Catholic, and two Jewish families were in residence at that time
(the early seventies).

The first recorded religious meeting was informal. On December
3, 1972, George and Corinne Van Kleeck, Dr. Roy Herndon, and Dorothy Saunders got together at the Cape Haze pool house to discuss the
spiritual needs of the residents.

Reaching quick agreement, they put a tiny classified advertisement
in the *Sarasota Herald-Tribune*:

> Needed: Minister for Sunday
> Services at Rotonda West
> Community Church.

The ad ran on Monday, December 24, 1972, although the church
was not yet officially organized, or even named. In fact, there was no
church. The ad drew eight responses.

The first interdenominational church services were held on Sunday morning, January 14, 1973, at the Community Center.

Moving quickly, on January 30, 1973 a formal organizing meeting
was held by George and Corinne Van Kleeck, George C. Herring, Dorothy Saunders and David Pease. Pease had recently organized the United
Church of Christ in Englewood and offered to help the Rotonda group.
The name—Rotonda West Community Church—was chosen. A draft

charter and constitution were drawn and temporary officers were appointed: chairman of church facilities, Dr. Roy Herndon; church program chairman, George C. Herring; treasurer, Nancy Kiebler; secretary, Dorothy Saunders; music chairman, Alice Dennis; chairman of meetings, George Van Kleeck.

"These were busy, happy times," said Dorothy Saunders Cannon. "They were marvelous people, very interdenominational. I was a Methodist, my late husband, Mike, was Catholic. George Van Kleeck was a wonderful man. He really was the organizer of our first church. He could preach a sermon himself, even better than most preachers."

Often, the Van Kleecks would take the entire congregation back to their Caddy Road home for brunch.

By March 11, 1973, when thirty-six people attended the Community Church's interdenominational services—"services informal, dress optional, all ages invited"—the group was being led by various lay volunteers, and on occasion by local preachers such as Rev. Jack Otis of Englewood North's Church of Christ, a retired Baptist minister.

One year later, on March 7, 1974, the congregation chose Edison G. Brooker as their regular preacher. Brooker had been one of the eight who responded to the original advertisement in the *Herald-Tribune*. He became the church's full-time pastor in November 1976.

Brooker, according to the early members, was a man of "quiet dignity, keen sensitivity and understanding." He was a graduate of the Nyack Missionary College in New York and had a master's degree from Baylor University in Waco, Texas. He was ordained in 1959 in the interdenominational Christian and Missionary Alliance. Before coming to Rotonda he served the Alliance Community Church in Duluth, Minnesota, where he also had a daily radio program. Brooker later moved to a church in Waco and became active in the Billy Graham Crusade.

Pastor Brooker, his wife Jackie, and son Brian, moved into a Rotonda home on Oakland Hills Court. Jackie became a supervisor at the First National Bank of Englewood, and Brian later joined the United States Navy.

During the first six months of 1974, average attendance at Community Church services was thirty-six. By 1976, attendance had risen to fifty-eight, with as many as one hundred during the winter season.

As the church became more active, it supported programs to involve Rotonda's young people, and missionary work done by Clinton and Barbara Padgett in Costa Rica.

However, viable as the nondenominational church quickly became, other groups wanted churches for their own faiths. One group formed Faith Lutheran Church.

Faith's first worship service was held on November 11, 1973, led by Carl Kaltreider, a Lutheran mission developer and by now a Rotonda resident.

11.1 Pastor Carl Kaltreider at first worked out of his Rotonda home.

Among the many involved with the start-up of Faith Lutheran were Harry and Harriet Virtue. "I made the first altar," Harry said. He recalled that there were about fourteen people in the early Faith group. They also made a survey of those attending the Lutheran church. "It seemed there were more Catholics than anything else," Virtue said, "but we wanted to get a church of our own started, so we prevailed on Carl Kaltreider to lead us." Which was, of course, why Kaltreider had been sent by the Lutheran church to Rotonda in the first place.

During 1973, the Faith group's service committee was active. On the committee were Mert Bowers, Loraine Gilcher, Frank Goodnight,

Wally Peterson, Sandy Rafeld and Harry Virtue. Pastor Kaltreider was temporary chairman.

In these days, Harry and Harriet Virtue remember, the Community Center was becoming a hive of religious activity on weekends . . . "first the Catholics, then the interdenominational [Community Church] group, then the Lutherans," said Harry.

"We all used the same hymnals, Methodist hymnals. We were all one big happy family."

Pastor Kaltreider had arrived in Rotonda in June 1973, "to develop a congregation in the Lutheran Church," as he put it. With his wife Patricia, son Jeff, and daughter Kitty, he came from Farmington, Michigan, where he had also been active with the Association of Christian Athletes.

A cheerfully outgoing man, Kaltreider was a graduate of Wittenberg University who studied later in Paris and at Queens College in Oxford, England. He was ordained in Grand Rapids in 1950. Pastor Carl, as he became known, served as chaplain to the "Superstars" when that television program started at Rotonda in 1973. On one occasion, in February 1974, Kaltreider persuaded America's preeminent soccer star, Kyle Rote, Jr. to preach the Sunday sermon. By all accounts, Rote was a smash hit.

"When I came to Rotonda," Kaltreider recalls "there were only about a hundred seventy-five residents. Sometimes I felt like pastor, priest and rabbi combined."

While the two churches competed for members they worked together in behalf of the community's spiritual needs. Easter, Thanksgiving, and New Year's Eve watchnight services were held jointly, one pastor preaching, the other leading the liturgy.

When the churches started up in the early 1970s, their services were held at various places, sometimes at the Riverhouse Condominiums poolhouse, or at Pike's Restaurant, which had opened for business in February 1973, on Cape Haze Drive at Kendall Road.

Eventually, as the groups became larger, which they did rapidly, Cavanagh allowed them to use the Community Center, which both churches then shared with the Catholic group for their weekend services. All three groups held mid-week Bible study in various private homes.

By the late 1970s the faithful were seeking their own church facilities and had formed building committees and started building funds. Eventually, after much discussion, six acres on Rotonda Boulevard West were donated by the developer for church buildings for the Community Church and Faith Lutheran Church. The Catholics were also offered three acres, but later decided to move out of the circle, a short drive up Placida Road.

Construction on the Community and Faith churches finally began in 1979, after three or four years of meetings and planning.

Pushing for the Community Church was a building committee led by Ray Gile and including G. C. Herring, Joe Brower, chairman of the church board, Edward Will, senior elder, and Pastor Brooker.

The church was built by ERB Building Systems. Its vaulted ceiling keeps it comfortable year-round. Entering the church from the Florida sunlight gives immediate relief, as if a cool blanket was wrapped around the head and shoulders. The building seats three hundred and is decorated with attractive beige and gold furnishings. It has an organ and a piano, employs a modern sound system, has an operational kitchen and several small teaching rooms.

Construction of the new church building on Rotonda Boulevard West was under way during the last six months of 1979. Eventually the building was completed. The last interdenominational service in the Community Center was held February 3, 1980. One week later, Sunday, February 10, the first service was held in the new building. It was "a joyous occasion, with 256 seats occupied." A congratulatory letter from President Jimmy Carter was read. Congressman John J. Duncan of Tennessee, brother-in-law of Helen Gile, addressed the congregation. Special thanks were given to Cape Cave Corporation's management for the unrestricted use of the community center during the formative years of the church. It had taken the determined faithful only eight years to get their church.

Meanwhile, in 1974, Faith opened its membership charter, the first step towards organizing their congregation. In May that year they formally elevated Kaltreider from mission developer to pastor. By 1975 the Faith Lutheran Church was on a solid footing, that year adopting its first budget: $18,549.

Dick Marshall recalls that when Faith decided to build a church, "We contacted the church hierarchy up north. They offered to put up $30,000 if our congregation would match it. At the time we had about thirty-five members." Dick and Mary Jane Marshall had come to Rotonda in 1977 from New Brunswick, New Jersey. They immediately became involved with the church.

By June 1978, Faith's building campaign was a success with $33,839 donated or pledged, and final plans for the building were completed. The estimated cost of the building was $210,000, a pittance where faith is concerned. In May 1980, Faith Church was dedicated after six months of construction by N. McAllister Contracting, Inc.

The church's well-known Schulmerich carillon bells had been installed earlier that month. The bells have a two-mile range and the music of their chimes peals across the Cape Haze peninsula on Sundays and special occasions.

The first service in the Faith Church was actually a Catholic Mass, according to Ed Melton. Ed and June Melton were charter members of the Faith Lutheran Church.

"We had about twenty-five people at first," Ed recalls. "Later, after our church building was finished, the Catholics had their Saturday night Mass in our building. Two Catholic nuns were there. One said to me, 'We've come a long way . . . years ago I wouldn't even have spoken to you.'"

There was one glitch involving the building of the new churches. When the brand new structures were finished they couldn't be used right away. They had no water, and therefore were denied the necessary county certificate of occupancy.

Bob Antes was on the Community Church building committee. He said there were many horror stories involved with the building of the church, availability of water being one. He said that dealing with the developer was continually frustrating. (By mid-1976, management of Rotonda had been assumed by Deltona Corporation. Kurt Schramm was Deltona's on-site manager.)

"Schramm was our contact," Antes said. "We told him in detail about our church-building plans so they would be ready to provide the church with potable water. We got closer and closer to completion and still no water."

At that stage, Rotonda West's water and sewer lines were still no closer than the intersection of Boundary and Rotonda West Boulevards, a quarter-mile from the church site.

"We knew we couldn't get the necessary certificate of occupancy without water," Antes said. "So we went to the County Commission. Thankfully, [Commissioner] Joe Tringali got us permission to function without the certificate. We had to pump water out of the pond to flush the toilets. For months we had signs — DON'T DRINK THIS WATER — all over the place."

Hugh Sumrall, Rotonda West Utility Corporation's project manager, reported completion of the water lines to both churches in August 1981, eighteen months after the buildings were ready for use.

Finally they had water. Although it certainly wasn't a miracle, "I'm delighted," said Pastor Brooker. "We'll use the water with appreciation."

Faith Church, next door, had suffered the same deprivation, and Pastor Kaltreider agreed that the new water lines were a welcome and necessary addition to his church.

Meanwhile, as the Community and Faith Churches were moving from dream to reality, Rotonda's Catholics had been far from idle.

During the early years they had been content to have Father Sebastian Loncar from St. Raphael's Catholic Church in Englewood visit Rotonda to minister to their needs. Actually, during the early 1970s, Rotonda's Catholic residents had been meeting at various places, the Community Center, then the theater in Palm Plaza, and finally at Lemon Bay High School.

By November 1975, the Catholic social hour at the Community Center was drawing one hundred twenty of the faithful, attended by Father Loncar. As had the other faiths, the Catholic contingent wanted their own place in which to worship.

Yolanda Leone, Robert O'Keefe and Sam Ferro met frequently to discuss ways to expand Catholic services in the community.

Jack LaBar was also an active Catholic. "There was a fairly large contingent of Catholics," he said. "At the time we were considered part of St. Raphaels. On our own, we had gotten three acres of land from Cavanagh to build our own church. Then the diocese in St. Petersburg got into the act in behalf of this whole area. It turned out they (the diocese) already had the land. Our land wasn't big enough anyway. The diocese wasn't looking just at Rotonda but at West Charlotte County as a whole."

Eventually, Rotonda's Catholics were satisfied. St. Francis of Assisi Catholic Church broke ground in nearby Grove City in February 1980. The ceremony was attended by Pastors Brooker and Kaltreider from Rotonda, and the church was completed, on eight acres on County Road 775, and dedicated November 27, 1980. Father Michael Cottrell was priest.

It had taken more than two years of planning and hoping but the result pleased Rotonda's Catholics, most of whom attended the dedication Mass. Charles and Mildred Kraft, and Rocky and Fran Rokisky were among them. Charles Kraft was then the Alcalde of the Fiesta Association, and Fran was president of the Rotonda Woman's Club.

And so, as with Rotonda's early social needs, its religious needs were met, over an incredibly brief eight-year period, due to the dedication and energy of many of Rotonda's early residents.

Now, if only they could get their mail delivered.

Playing Post Office

I N FEBRUARY 1972, a small post office opened at Rotonda. Before that, the residents went to Placida to the tiny post office by The Fishery Seafood Market. The new unit was housed in a section of the deli on Cape Haze Drive by the Texaco gas station. It would operate as a sub-station of Placida and Mike Saunders, aided by his wife Dorothy, would be the Rotonda postmaster.

By October 1973 the postmaster had to plead with the residents not to come for their mail before 10 A.M. to give them time to sort what had quickly became a deluge of mail, up to 1,500 pieces daily, five times the volume it had handled when it first opened.

First resident Joan Kaar also worked in the sub-station, although she had come South to retire. "But," she said, reasonably, "Mike and Dorothy needed help."

Kaar remembers the sub-station as a friendly place. There was no home delivery then, so everyone had to come to pick up or deliver mail. "I got to know everyone that way," Kaar said.

On May 19, 1975, the Placida post office started curbside delivery in Rotonda West. Needless to say, concern was immediately expressed about the standards of beauty of the mailboxes, and recommendations for standard mailboxes were offered in Ethel Furia's *Bulletin*. These could be purchased at Babe's Hardware, Taylor Rental or through the Sears Roebuck Catalog, said the *Bulletin*. Cost: from $13.39 to $18.40.

Of greater concern to the community of Placida was the suspicion that their little post office, an historical landmark which had opened in 1900, was about to be relocated to Rotonda.

It was not the first post office to be moved. After World War ll, the entire community of Gasparilla, along with its post office, was relocated from the north end of Gasparilla Island to Placida.

The hysteria about the possible new location in Rotonda was captured in an *Englewood Herald* article, run under an ominous five-column headline: "Placida Fights to Halt P.O. Shift to Rotonda."

"Embattled citizens of Placida," it began, conjuring up a picture of Placida residents hunkered down inside their mobile-homes waiting to slay the postmaster general "belying the placid name of their picturesque little village . . . voted to fight to the finish to keep their postal facility in Placida and prevent its removal to Rotonda West."

Petitions were circulated and forwarded to Congress. An investigation was demanded. One key to the furor was Postmaster General Elmer T. Klassen's house in Rotonda. Said one Placida resident, "We're going to make it our business to learn . . . if this has anything to do with the proposal to move our postal service to Rotonda."

The situation was aggravated when it was learned that the Placida postmaster, Don Scaggs, not only recommended the move but was even considering a Rotonda home for himself.

"You're going to have a fight, young man," one Placidan yelled. "We don't intend to let these birds come in here and tell us we're going to have our post office up there."

The ire of the one hundred plus citizens attending the session at Gasparilla Mobile Estates rose to a crescendo when Scaggs told them he made his recommendation believing that, within ten years, the bulk of the area population would live in Rotonda. At the time of the meeting the post office was serving two hundred seventy-eight Placida residents and only two hundred eighteen in Rotonda. But Rotonda was slated to have an eventual twenty thousand residents, Scaggs noted.

Cape Haze residents were equally indignant. "Cape Haze will never allow their mail to come through Rotonda," one said flatly, reflecting a polarization that still seems to exist between Rotonda and Cape Haze.

The Cape Haze attitude toward them has always annoyed Rotondans. Now they were surprised, having thought a truce had been reached between both sides of County Road 775. Said one newspaper story, "Recently, Cape Haze residents signed a truce in a long fought battle with Rotonda over use of private beaches and numerous other issues. These became bones of contention following the purchase of Rotonda and adjoining properties from Alfred and William Vanderbilt."

Meanwhile, Rotonda's sub-station was terminated. Joan Kaar went to work at Placida and eventually became its postmaster. She would later move over to the Boca Grande post office. So much for her planned retirement.

The Rotonda West Property Owners Association (POA) newsletter conceded, October 10, 1975, "We lost the fight to keep our post office open. However, we shall reopen the fight at a later date, when we are large enough to convince the postal service to build in Rotonda."

That day wouldn't come until eighteen years later, in 1993, when the Placida post office closed and a new state-of-the-art post office was opened on County Road 775, near the Rotonda/Cape Haze entrances. It is still called the Placida post office—it seems the federal authorities didn't want the expense of changing all the nation's telephone directories to reflect "Rotonda post office."

And so the game of post office went on.

Superstars

ASK ROTONDANS to recall their most vivid memories of the early 1970s and inevitably "The Superstars" will be mentioned. It seems that Olympic skater Dick Button had dreamed for years of a program where international sports stars would compete, head-to-head, in any five out of ten sports—other than their own. In one aspect, "The Superstars" suggested the Olympic decathlon idea— a contest to determine the super-athlete.

The year Button won the Sullivan Award as the top athlete in the United States, he said in a press interview, "I knew there were at least ten guys who could beat me in just about everything."

With this modest admission Button began thinking about a unique sporting event, and The Superstars[3] was conceived.

Button owned "The Superstars." He became wealthy from his concept when it was televised in the United States and more wealthy when it was expanded with events around the world. Later, it was broadened further to embrace female sports stars. Eventually even celebrities were shown acting out their sports fantasies. The viewing public loved it.

No question, the picture of Cincinnati Reds catcher Johnny Bench playing tennis, or the NFL's Franco Harris competing in a bicycle race, had undeniable appeal.

When Button and his business associate, Paul Feigay, brought the idea to Barry Frank of Trans World International, Inc. (TWI), it quickly became reality. TWI was the production arm of Mark McCormack's powerful International Management Group (IMG). Frank himself was top-rated in the management of professional athletes, and had the expertise to convey the excitement of sports through the electronic media.

At the time—it was 1972, and Rotonda West was just getting roll-ing—ABC-TV was preeminent in sports telecasting, so Frank took the idea to them. It was agreed the concept had weekend viewer potential, but an advertising sponsor was vital to the plan, so Bob Perlstein of SFM Media Services was invited in. SFM associates began to pitch the idea, and finally sold it to the marketing brass at the Fram Automobile Division of Fram Corporation.

13.1 Ed McMahon chats with sportscaster Jim McKay during the ABC "Superstars" events. Baseball hero Johnny Bench looks on.

The chain was now almost complete—an appealing sports idea, someone to fund it, and a major network to televise it. Now a suitable site was needed.

An intensive search was mounted. The obvious requirements included weather that could be relied upon, and sports facilities adequate to stage such disparate events as track and bowling, swimming and tennis, cycling and rowing.

The site search has been described in newspaper accounts as "exhaustive." Whether or not Rotonda's developer lobbied in Rotonda's behalf is unknown. Suffice to say Rotonda was finally selected, and Joe Klein seemed delighted that his unique new community was about to enjoy nationwide television exposure on sports telecasts, weekend after weekend. Indeed, Rotonda West was placed firmly on the national map as the "Birthplace of 'The Superstars.'"

13.2 ABC's "Superstars" events in progress at Rotonda West, about 1973.

Having approved the event, ABC's Roone Arledge tapped his dynamic young sports producer, Don Ohlmeyer, for the task of getting "The Superstars" "in the can" for weekend telecasting. Ohlmeyer had won five Emmy Awards for his work and was enthusiastic about the idea.

"Don was a close friend of our son, Bill," said Rotondan June Melton. "He used to come to the house when he was here, walking in the door asking, 'What's for dinner?' " She also remembers, "We were all involved in 'The Superstars.' We'd get up at six-thirty every morning, fix the coffee and set out the doughnuts, hot dogs and hamburgers."

Bill and Catherine George, who came to Rotonda in 1974 from Hamilton, Ohio, operated a hot dog stand. "It was great fun," Kate George said. "A great way to meet our new neighbors."

With all planning completed, "The Superstars" program was launched. On February 19, 20, and 21, 1973, the first events were held at Rotonda. They were to be viewed on February 25 as a two-hour,

$122,000 sports TV special. The pictorial backdrop was, of course, Rotonda West. Great exposure.

Joe Klein had already declared, on behalf of Cavanagh Communities Corporation, that Ed McMahon, as their vice-president of community relations, was the official host of "The Superstars." The impression was left that McMahon would entertain the athletes with cocktail parties and dinners at his sumptuous new home in Rotonda West's Oakland Hills subdivision.

For his part, supersalesman McMahon publicly blessed Florida Governor Reubin Askew's proclamation—The week of February 18 to 25, 1973, was officially "Superstars Week in Florida."

The press, as might be expected, had a field day with "The Superstars." Much to Cavanagh's delight, Rotonda figured prominently in the deluge of publicity, as "The Home of 'The Superstars' " . . . where a beautiful sequence of dreams is turning into a living reality."

Publicity can be magnified, of course, where controversy exists, and "The Superstars" was immediately controversial. The program sparked fierce debate in both television and sports circles—was this real sport, or just entertainment? Dick Button believed this was sport, that his program would prove that an authentic athlete could handle himself well in events other than his own specialty. Critics hated the idea of a sports hero like tennis immortal Rod Laver, for example, floundering in a swimming race.

As the debate flared on, however, few would deny that the ultimate winner had to be a superb, multi-talented athlete.

Before the start-up of "The Superstars," Cavanagh crews had worked hard to finish the necessary facilities, some of which had to be constructed especially for the program.

"We had to hurry our construction on some things that normally wouldn't have been completed in such short time," said Jim Petrides, Cavanagh's on-site project manager. In fact, "The Superstars" had Cavanagh's crews working round the clock for a month. Needless to say, this raised some hackles.

"They never worked this hard building our homes," observed one Rotondan.

Nor was money a problem. Cavanagh threw over a million dollars into the project. The money went into completion of the Riverhouse

Condominium complex, where the athletes would be housed, an Olympic pool, the PGA-rated Sunday golf course, and, in Rotonda Shores, a thirty-six-acre park containing a hard-surface track and field oval suited for running and biking, canals (which now featured signs warning "Beware of Alligators") to be used for rowing events, a baseball diamond and the state-of-the-art professional (but portable—it could be installed in the Community Center only when needed) bowling alley.

The Riverhouse complex was completed in February 1973, just in time to house the stars, the media, and the ABC-TV production crew. Built facing the Rotonda River, it comprised seventeen individual buildings—each with eight one-or-two-bedroom apartments, individually priced from $34,500 to $41,000. So, on to the games.

Branch Rickey, Jr., a well known and respected baseball name, served as chief umpire overall. Cavanagh got into the act by naming Capt. Stephen B. Archer, U.S. Navy, (ret.), as on-site event coordinator.

The events in which the athletes competed—they were all men at first—were tennis, golf, swimming, bowling, weightlifting, baseball-hitting, a one-mile bike race, table tennis, a half-mile run and a one hundred-yard sprint. Rowing (on the Rotonda River) was later added and table tennis was dropped.

The athletes who initiated this unique new sports show read like a *Who's Who* in international sports at the time. Included were Johnny Bench, baseball; Joe Frazier, boxing; Rod Gilbert, ice hockey; Elvin Hayes, basketball; Rod Laver, tennis; Jean-Claude Killy, skiing; Bob Seagren, pole vaulting; Peter Revson, auto racing; Johnny Unitas, football; and Jim Stefanich, bowling.

That Barry Frank and his group could pull together such an illustrious roster for an untried, unknown event was truly remarkable. Unitas and Laver, for example, were arguably the best ever in their respective sports. Hayes was a star of magnitude, Killy was both the preeminent skier of his day and certainly the most charismatic. Frazier would become boxing's world champion. Bench made the baseball Hall of Fame.

These were athletes of legend. Obviously they took a gamble getting involved in "The Superstars." Professional reputations were at stake here; an injury could sideline an athlete in his chosen sport, even terminate a lucrative career. Yet for each, the allure of nationwide television exposure, plus a dose of the kind of pride that stokes a professional athlete's ego, brought them out.

Rotondan Charles Toops said, "I think, at first, they thought it was all in fun. Later, when '[The] Superstars' became a big success, they would train hard for it."

There was prize money to be won, of course, over $122,000 in the initial "Superstars" event. Plus residuals of contracts for television, potential commercials, appearances and endorsements. As "The Superstars" television program expanded in scope in later years to include female athletes, then celebrities, the prize money came to exceed $1 million. Not bad money at the time.

13.3 Sportscasting legend Howard Cosell interviews Hall of Fame NFL running back, O. J. Simpson, during "The Superstars" events at Rotonda.

Making sure that Rotonda West got adequate exposure from "The Superstars," Cavanagh President Joe Klein personally presented each athlete with a Rotonda lot. For some time thereafter rumors proliferated that pole vaulter Bob Seagren actually planned to build and live in Rotonda, next door to Ed McMahon in Oakland Hills. He never did.

Many of the stars came to Rotonda early for the event. Bench, for example, spent several days filming television commercials on Don Pedro Island. These were televised during the program.

In the first event, Seagren not only proved his athletic prowess by winning outright, he charmed everyone involved with his friendly, unpretentious manner. Seagren picked up $39,700 for his forty-nine-point victory. Skier Killy was second.

In subsequent years—"The Superstars" remained at Rotonda for five years, from 1973 to 1977—male winners would include soccer star Kyle Rote, Jr., and O. J. Simpson, who beat out both Seagren and Rote. Rote also won a second time, winning over football star Lynn Swann.

The sport versus entertainment debate notwithstanding, the element of showmanship was evident. Some participants demonstrated that idols can have athletic feet of clay yet still enjoy being human. Prizefighter Joe Frazier, for example, floundered, laughing uproariously, in his swimming event. Unitas, doing his famous backwards shuffle to receive a tennis lob, seemed surprised to find a racquet in his hand instead of a pigskin. Several bowlers rolled scores embarrassingly below one hundred, while several golf scores exceeded the national debt. Spectators watched delightedly as Franco Harris belted twelve golf balls in succession into a Rotondan's back yard.

Surprisingly, Bob Seagren would beat muscle man Frazier in weightlifting. Frazier caved in at one hundred-seventy pounds. In later events, Mr. Universe, Lou Ferrigno, had to go to two hundred fifty-five pounds to beat Preston Pearson of the Dallas Cowboys.

So "The Superstars" went, Rotonda residents enjoying the entire spectacle close-up and personal while helping out, trying to be captured in a television shot, and telling the folks back home how wonderful Rotonda was.

"If you were sports-minded you couldn't fail to enjoy it," said ex-New York cop, John Lawson. "A few stars were full of ego and wouldn't sign autographs, but most of them were great."

Rotonda residents helped throughout. Ed Will and Bob MacDonald served as tennis umpires; Pastor Kaltreider manned the scoreboard; Rotonda kids caddied, including Joe Furia, Bill Hyde, G. C. Manyak, Dan Shields, Jeff Kaltreider, C. Horton, and G. Thornton.

Helping flag baseball hits for distance were Lucille Hall, Charlie Kraft and Helen Spitzmueller. G. C. Herring was a starter for track events; and other timers and judges included Silvio Furia, Bill Phillips, Fred Parmalee, Adam Walters and Jim Lamorte. Most residents did something, serving as marshals or manning refreshment tables. Many said they could pick themselves out of TV background shots.

Whether or not it was a sports success, "The Superstars" was a television hit. It ran at Rotonda through 1977. It brought to Rotonda the likes of Roger Staubach, Dick Anderson, Carl Eller and Franco Harris (football); Stan Smith and Arthur Ashe (tennis); track stars Brian Oldfield, Lee Evans, Jim Ryun, and decathlon star Bill Toomey.

From the baseball circuit came Jim Palmer, Brooks Robinson, Tug McGraw, Pete Rose and Reggie Jackson; auto racers Jody Scheckter, Craig Breedlove, Emerson Fitipaldi and Bobby Allison; and basketball pros John Havlicek, Nate Archibald and Jim McMillan.

Others included Bill Muncy (hydroplane racing); swimmers Don Schollander and Mike Burton; Gene Morero (motorcycling); Misha Petkevitch (figure skating); Dan Gable (wrestling); hockey stars Stan Mikita and Brad Park; even rodeo legend Larry Mahan.

13.4 Sprinter Wyomia Tyus and tennis star Martina Navratilova watching other world-class athletes compete at "The Superstars."

To the delight of the Rotondans, divinity student and soccer player, Kyle Rote, Jr., emerged as the second winner. He and his wife Mary Lynn gave away most of his $53,400 winning purse to charity.

Most of the athletes mingled with the "locals" during television shooting delays. "Real charmers" by all accounts were Rote, Seagren and O. J. Simpson. And Laver was labeled "a perfect gentleman."

The women liked Bench, and "there wasn't a nicer person than John Havlicek." Billy Jean King and Reggie Jackson, however, came across as prima donnas with large egos. Later, when "The Superstars" expanded to include celebrities, "there was one," said John Lawson, "an excellent actor, who was terribly full of himself."

But most stars are warmly remembered. Ethel Furia said, "When O. J. Simpson came, a group of kids, not from here, followed him around shouting, 'O. J.! O. J.!' "

Much of O. J.'s wealth and success resulted from when he was seen on "The Superstars" in 1975 by an executive of Ted Bates & Company, a New York ad agency seeking an athlete for Hertz, according to Kara Swisher, writing in *Washington Post Weekly* (July 1994). O. J. was signed by Hertz for $200,000 a year for three years. This grew to $550,000 a year, and the Hertz connection—initiated when O. J. was seen performing at Rotonda—brought him other quality endorsement contracts, and an income that exceeded $1 million a year before his startling arrest for murder in June 1994.

Ed Hennessey volunteered as a driver. "I drove O. J. down from Tampa," he recalled. "I went back the next day to pick up his [first] wife and two little children. Their luggage never came through. They spent three days without it because it was stored at another airline."

"Billy ('White Shoes') Johnson [NFL football], taught Sunday School," said Pastor Kaltreider. "So did Kyle Rote. And Franco Harris worked with our children. When rain canceled a bike race, O. J. and others spent hours just chatting with us. We even debated Noah and the ark and the story of Adam and Eve. They just endeared themselves to us." Even ABC-TV's veteran sports announcer Keith Jackson was acknowledged as "a super guy, really great."

Helen Waldron said, "Cavanagh really spent money on this. Of course they were making it hand over fist. They had a big tent for the athletes, and gave us chits for food too."

Rotondans also got complimentary passes, vehicle identification decals, and most sported "Rotonda Superstars" bumper stickers. The kids had cards on their bikes and school binders.

The athletes themselves often ate at Pike's Restaurant, on Cape Haze Drive, which ultimately became the first home of Rotonda's Elks.

"The food was super," said Ray Edelstein. "They had no liquor license but Cavanagh gave it away liberally. We'd sneak in there sometimes, and if we sat down there'd be a bottle of wine in front of us in a minute."

Wesley Olson, then working for Cape Cave Corporation, found himself assigned as property manager for "The Superstars" events. "We moved equipment from place to place," Olson said. "It was fun getting to know the athletes. My daughters thoroughly enjoyed it."

Early residents Charles and Rosemary Toops saw every event over the program's five-year span at Rotonda. "We worked the booths," Charles said, "and watched and yelled encouragement to the competitors when they performed."

No doubt about it, "The Superstars" melded the new community. As they arrived, new residents became caught up in it, "everyone getting involved, meeting each other and helping out with a community-minded spirit," said Rosemary Toops.

In the mid-1970s, the show expanded. Suddenly, female sports stars became familiar sights at Rotonda. They included skater Ann Henning; golfers Jane Blalock and Amy Alcott; track stars Lacy O'Neal and Wyomia Tyus; drag-racer Shirley Muldowny; volleyball's Mary Jo Peppler; and tennis stars Martina Navratilova, Billie Jean King and Althea Gibson.

In 1975 Peppler won, with $34,100 in the prize kitty. In 1976 Henning dominated, winning $51,400.

Later, celebrity stars showed their athletic abilities. They included Robert Duvall (known for his roles in the films *Godfather* and *Lonesome Dove*); Kent McCord ("Adam 12"); fashion designer Oleg Cassini; George Lindsey ("Hee Haw"); authors Peter Benchley (*Jaws*) and George Plimpton (*Paper Lion*); pianist Peter Duchin; country singer Kenny Rogers, and actors Bruce Dern, Rob Reiner, and Michael Dante. Duvall won.

Cincinnati Reds catcher Bench summed up the professional athletes' attitude to "The Superstars." He said, "I'm competing in tennis, golf, swimming, bowling, and the bike race. I'm here to give all I've got. After all, I'm representing baseball."

As for the worldwide publicity gained by Rotonda, Joe Klein said, "We're enthralled with the event. Public reaction has been outstanding. We may have 'Superstars' for another ten years."

Klein could hope. Cavanagh had a ten-year contract with ABC-TV, but the show ran only five years at Rotonda, then went elsewhere, seeking broader television coverage.

Organizing for Defense

1972 AND 1973 were formative years for Rotonda as transplanted Northerners began fresh lives in their new environment. The early residents reached out to each other for mutual support. The social whirl revved up as new clubs and associations took root. "The Superstars" created a euphoria; it was exciting rubbing shoulders with internationally renowned sports figures and celebrities.

Despite the trauma many experienced getting into their new homes— even, in some cases, getting their homes built—the early consensus on Rotonda was favorable. Well, almost.

One resident, Joe Ryan, was quoted in the *Sarasota Herald-Tribune* during "The Superstars" period as saying "Lots of us here are sick and tired of what the company keeps promising but never delivering." Ryan said he had submitted sixty-four complaints about his new house.

In a news interview, resident John Larsen claimed Cavanagh "failed to live up to promises." Larsen owned eight lots in The Shores and Pine Valley, both undeveloped sections of Rotonda. "The undeveloped state of the properties made them impossible [to use]," Larsen said, adding, "There's no evidence of any progress whatsoever." He also said he owned the lots outright but was paying utility assessments of two hundred dollars a month on them and doubted if the land was worth the taxes he paid.

Others were beginning to sense that Cavanagh was an uncaring developer, one uninterested in the residents' needs and continually failing to perform to expectations. *The Vision* was already fading.

What happened next was inevitable. About forty residents got together, informally, determined to defend their mutual interests. In a free-for-all discussion they expressed their concerns about Cavanagh policies and performance.

On November 23, 1973, a letter was circulated. It began "Dear Homeowner," and floated the idea of a homeowners association "to seek improvement of the many conditions which currently appear to be deteriorating the appearance of our new community."

This precursor of a wave of complaints that later overtook Cavanagh first focused on the relatively insignificant matter of trash—at that stage the "Number One" aggravation. And, as an offshoot of that, the comportment of Cavanagh's work crews who were blamed for the trash. "We are surrounded with trash and garbage," the letter declared. "We are bothered by vandalism, rowdyism, speeding trucks and heavy equipment. Workmen's cars trample our lawns. Loose dogs violate our shrubs."

Almost as an afterthought, Cavanagh's performance in maintaining the roads, completing the canals and keeping up the golf course was also criticized.

The letter sought to establish a formal, legally competent organization that would "pool our resources and present a united front," and ensure the rights of its members. An organizational meeting was scheduled for Sunday, December 9, 1973, at the Community Center.

The letter was signed by the ad hoc committee spawned at the earlier informal gripe session. Five names—J. A. Tringali, chairman; Carl Kaltreider, secretary; Charles Kraft, treasurer; John Allison and Bill Phillips—gave it credibility.

Specific complaints listed in the letter included: no security system, no guardhouse and road barrier at the County Road 775 entrance to Rotonda as promised; eggs and tomatoes thrown at homes; one resident's name sign thrown into a canal; vandals breaking windows and starting fires in homes under construction; widespread theft of appliances, cabinets and carpeting from homes almost completed but still not occupied.

The letter noted that these and related problems had been laid before Cavanagh's vice-president, Marshall Ames.

"I am convinced," said Tringali, "that without . . . the pressure of our committee . . . cleanup would not have begun so quickly."

News of the organizing effort was widely reported in Englewood, Punta Gorda, and Sarasota news media that covered Charlotte County.

Feelings obviously ran high. Phillips had immediate second thoughts and resigned almost before the letter was issued. One news story claimed that Tringali's home was "cherry-bombed" in early January 1974.

One resident, Fred Parmalee, sent a letter to the newspapers criticizing their coverage, and disavowing some of Tringali's statements. "Many of the statements [in the press] are not in accord with the feelings of many home owners," Parmalee wrote. "Some who have lived here since the beginning were not allowed to comment on the charges."

Tringali responded in print. "Has he [Parmalee] not been bothered by roaring motorcycles racing through our streets? Does he know that . . . my home was vandalized by thrown cherry bombs and firecrackers that scarred our house and startled my neighbors?"

As the idea of a homeowners' association took hold it became obvious that trash, while an annoyance, was the least of the residents' concerns.

"Where is the promised country club?" they asked. They referred to a quote by Joe Klein in Cavanagh's 1971 annual report about the clubhouse: "completion of this magnificent structure is scheduled for May 31, 1973." But it was already 1973 and the clubhouse wasn't started yet.

Tringali also noted a quote in *Golf Digest* by Jim Petrides that the second golf course would be opened by January 1974. There was no evidence of work on that, either. (In fact, it wouldn't be ready for another fifteen years).

Summing up, Tringali stressed the need for homeowners to band together to have more clout with both Cavanagh and county authorities.

Cavanagh quickly acknowledged the movement, but was obviously stung by the publicity. Marshall Ames declared, "The company recognizes that creation of such a group is not only inevitable but desirable, as long as it works in concert with the company." In a more caustic vein Ames continued, "This message was going to be one of welcome and support . . . [but] I can think of no other way to cut the lines of communication between the company and such an organization than to begin a program of accusations and vilification in the local newspapers." Ames concluded on a sour note, "I am not convinced that a formally organized association is necessary."

The organizing continued. The December 9, 1973, meeting at the Community Center attracted ninety-seven homeowners. Tringali was applauded when he outlined the aims and objectives for the group. A vote recorded approval by ninety-four of those attending, with three dissenting. A committee was formed on the spot to develop a constitution, bylaws, a plan of action and a slate of officers. Headed by Tringali, the committee included Don Zeigler, Charles Toops, Helen Allison and Cliff McCauley.

On March 10, 1974, residents were informed by mail that the Rotonda West Property Owners Association (RWPOA[4]) was a fact. The letter was signed by Joseph A. Tringali, president. It invited residents and lot owners to join. Annual dues were $10 up front for residents, plus $2.50 per quarter. Non-residents would pay half that amount. By July the POA had 164 paid-up members, 131 residents and 33 non-residents.

14.1 By 1974, Oakland Hills began to show signs of home building.

It is obvious that without Joe Tringali, Rotonda would be less well off today.

"The POA was an absolute necessity," said Joe Obey, a future POA president. "It's the only watchdog the residents have that looks to their interests rather than the developer's . . . the only way to keep the developer in line."

Obey recalls how Tringali typed the early POA newsletters himself, ran them off on a ditto machine, hundreds of them, then had them delivered.

Jack Labar, who also would become POA president, said, "Among other things, the POA was involved in getting Lemon Bay [Junior High] upgraded to full high school status."

"Thank God for Joe Tringali," said George Manyak, a sentiment echoed by most of Rotonda's 1970s residents.

As a retired career army officer used to command and organization and things being accomplished efficiently, Tringali was a natural for the new POA. He was prepared to confront Cavanagh wherever the developer wasn't doing what it had promised. "I'd never been into anything political in my life," Tringali said. Maybe so, but he quickly got the POA organized, launched, active and forcing concessions from Cavanagh in the property owners' interests.

On Cavanagh's side the POA was an aggravation. The developer claimed the organization represented only a small minority of the property owners. The company resisted being coerced, causing Tringali to complain, "Why will they not discuss matters with us?"

Tringali pointed out that he had gone out of his way to cooperate with the developer—"I wrote an extremely conciliatory letter offering them the hand of friendship"—but Cavanagh didn't respond.

Once Jim Petrides, then Cavanagh's on-site manager, told Tringali that Cavanagh's president would meet with him but only as a resident. Cavanagh would not recognize the POA.

This flurry of positioning by the developer and the POA continued throughout 1974. In May, Tringali formally requested a meeting with Cavanagh management to discuss "problem areas."

These included the lack of a clubhouse—"it was promised"; care and maintenance of the golf course—"it's poorly maintained"; adequacy of water and sewage plant—"a matter of grave concern"; beautification of entrances, roadways and greenbelts—"far from the attractive place you promised."

There were other aggravations. Unpaved streets, unfinished canals, unbuilt bridges, lack of security, failure to replace trees and shrubs removed by work crews.

At last the president of Cape Cave, Joel Jankowitz, responded. He wrote, "I have directed James Petrides to get in touch with you to clarify the problems raised, and work out a program for their solution."

However, personable and cooperative as Petrides was, the confrontations went on during the balance of 1974 as new problems kept arising.

Street lighting was one. The county had created a county-wide street lighting district. Now all county residents had to pay their share of street lighting, whether or not they had lights in their own areas. In Rotonda, most did not.

On this one, Tringali showed evidence of his political instincts, having the POA support the county measure to help its passage, then demanding lights for Rotonda in early 1975.

Another concern was the state's proposal to downgrade State Road 775 to county status. This would put the road's upkeep on the county taxpayers. Said Tringali, "With Rotonda emerging as a major new community . . . the road should be improved rather than downgraded." It was downgraded.

By now it was obvious to Cavanagh that the POA and its issues wouldn't go away, but would compound the developer's already considerable problems.

Then, with the POA on a sound footing, Tringali raised his sights and ran for the Charlotte County Commission. He was elected in 1976, then later was reelected twice. From his county office he was of frequent help in matters bearing on Rotonda.

"If there hadn't been a Tringali and a POA things would have been very different around here," said Joe Obey, one of Tringali's successors as president of the POA.

Cavanagh's Problems Mount

CAVANAGH COMMUNITIES Corporation had several tigers by the tail. The selling of Rotonda was creating a cascade of money, but the company faced a cash-flow problem.

Cavanagh also was constantly in litigation during the early 1970s, and this concerned many property owners.

One early legal brawl stemmed from their failure to pay part of their mortgage, which was held by the Vanderbilts.

Attorney Leo Wotitzky, who had represented the Vanderbilts and negotiated the sale of their property to Cavanagh, said of the developer, "They had to sell lots, mostly on time, to make payments and get releases on the mortgage."

Wotitzky said the Vanderbilts had to foreclose on the last part of the mortgage, about $2.4 million. It covered some less desirable tracts of the property, "about three thousand acres as I recall," Wotitzky said.

The property in question was at the south end of Bull's Bay and Turtle Bay, essentially marginal land, partially under water, clearly undevelopable.

The foreclosure was later complicated when Cavanagh filed for bankruptcy. Wotitzky couldn't proceed without the approval of the bankruptcy court, which was in Boston. "So, we had to go to Boston . . . retain bankruptcy counsel . . . appear before the court and get permission to go forward with the foreclosure." They got it.

Attorney Guy Batsel was assigned to the Vanderbilts' foreclosure action. "It was the first large issue between the parties," Batsel said. Under the terms of the original mortgage the indebtedness could be retired against separate parcels in a selective way, pretty much as Cavanagh elected. "They decided not to pay the final couple of installments on the mortgage," he said. "I think they could have paid it, but then they went into bankruptcy."

It turned out that Joe Klein outsmarted himself in the matter. Before the foreclosure started, Leo Wotitzky had arranged for Cape Haze Water Company to be pledged as part of the security. "When the mortgage went into default, the first thing we did was take over [the water company] pretty summarily," Wotitzky said. The Vanderbilts still held the utility's stock.

Recalls Batsel, "This was a fairly risky legal strategy seizing the utility, literally taking possession of it." Batsel said there was case law to oppose such an action, but, although Cavanagh had competent counsel, their lawyers apparently didn't see any remedies, a fact that became pivotal in the negotiations that ensued.

Batsel remembers that William Vanderbilt, who was then living in Manasota Key, drove back and forth almost daily for about nine months and literally ran the utility with Jim Petrides, who then worked for the Vanderbilts.

Batsel chuckles at the memory. Here was Vanderbilt, the distinguished former governor of Rhode Island, driving a beat-up old Volkswagen that could hardly make it, controlling the utility's dispensation of potable water into Rotonda while Joe Klein gnashed his teeth.

In December 1974, Cavanagh had had enough negative local press and complaints from Rotonda residents. They issued a statement that the newspapers "may have misinterpreted" the impact of the mortgage foreclosure on Rotonda.

The statement declared, "After Cavanagh purchased 26,000 acres from the Vanderbilts in 1969, we determined that approximately 18,000 acres were economically developable."

Cavanagh claimed that mortgage releases were obtained for each area as it was platted in the 18,000-acre-parcel. This meant, they said, that the Vanderbilt mortgage did not cover Rotonda property which had been platted and sold.

The press had made it clear, however, that not only residents and lot purchasers needed reassurance, so did the county. So the Cavanagh statement went on to say, "In addition to the cash and performance bonds deposited with Charlotte County, multi-million dollar cash deposits have been placed in an improvement escrow." They pointed out that these funds could not be released without the approval of the Florida Division of Land Sales.

"Every monthly assessment payment received from contract holders by Cape Cave Corporation is deposited in that account," Cavanagh stated.

Nonetheless, everyone was relieved when, in 1975, Cavanagh caved in, completed all mortgage payments due, and the Vanderbilt foreclosure was withdrawn. "We let them buy back the water utility and gave them credit against the mortgage," Wotitzky said.

The "marginal" land that caused the problem was eventually sold to the state for over two million dollars, under the Environmentally Endangered Lands Act, a deal also negotiated by Leo Wotitzky.

Interestingly, Wotitzky agreed to represent Cavanagh when the Vanderbilt sale was completed. "They asked if I would represent them," Wotitzky said, "and I said I would if the Vanderbilts didn't object. I also said that if they got into default again or into any conflict with the Vanderbilts, I'd represent the Vanderbilts against them."

Wotitzky, therefore, was legal counsel to Cavanagh for a brief period, until, as he puts it, ". . . it became just totally untenable. The state started investigating them, then the Federal Trade Commission got into the act . . . the truth was I just didn't trust them . . . and I quit."

Then another bombshell. Joe Tringali, POA president, would tell his members on February 18, 1975, "Cavanagh is about to announce that it is seeking relief under Chapter 11 of the Bankruptcy Act."

The bankruptcy shook many residents who worried about the future of their new community, but in a show of unity they pitched in to help. After all, this was their community.

Ray Edelstein remembers, ". . . the club members would take a day to clean the golf course. We'd all bring lawn mowers and scour the course of palm fronds, pine cones and needles."

Tringali insisted that the Cavanagh bankruptcy did not involve its Cape Cave subsidiary, the engine that drove Rotonda.

"It doesn't mean the company will dissolve," he said. "They are merely seeking relief from their creditors to extend payment of their indebtedness."

An executive from the First National Bank of Tampa, representing the consortium of Cavanagh's lending banks and institutions, told the Charlotte County Commission, "We do not intend to abandon the

Rotonda project . . . it is considered a good one." The fact is that in its lifetime Rotonda never turned out "good" as bankers define the word. They all took a financial beating.

Meanwhile, still other problems had surfaced for the beleaguered developer.

An article appeared May 20, 1973, in the *Detroit News* suggesting that Cavanagh's sales tactics were excessively aggressive.

It seemed that a news reporter, in the guise of a potential buyer, had visited Rotonda and uncovered what he alleged was "a pattern of sales misrepresentation."

During a three-hour tour the posing reporter was assured that he could get an annual 25 percent return on a Rotonda lot investment . . . that U.S. Postmaster General Elmer T. Klassen owned a home in Rotonda and would bring a full-scale post office to the community . . . and, if he later regretted his purchase, that he could sell his lot back to the company. The paper cited a list of negative findings.

Responding to this adverse criticism Cavanagh dispatched Marshall Ames and Phillip Bottfeld, both Cape Cave vice-presidents, to a two-hour conference with the *Detroit News*.

"All these claims and promises are in conflict with Cavanagh policy," they declared, according to another story written by the *News'* Michael Wendland.

Wendland's article quoted Ames as saying that Cavanagh was proud of its reputation and offered a generous twelve-month refund period for buyers, and strove to resolve every complaint.

"Our organization makes upwards of 80,000 sales presentations a year, some complaints are inevitable," Ames said.

Bottfeld was quoted admitting that he was disturbed by various government agencies that regulate land developers for citing Cavanagh as being among the leaders in the number of consumer complaints generated.

The executives told the *Detroit News* that their company deliberately played down the fact that Postmaster Klassen was a Rotonda resident and that television's Ed McMahon was its official spokesman.

Much had been made of McMahon's appointment as a corporate executive and his building a house in Oakland Hills, facts always stressed by Cavanagh salesmen.

"McMahon is a strong believer in Rotonda," Bottfeld said, adding, "however, we do not imply in any of our advertising that he actually lives on the site. After all, he's a busy man."

Interestingly, both executives told the *Detroit News* that Rotonda would be developed just as the company had promised. Ames said he couldn't give specific dates for completion, but "we're not just selling land, we're building a community." The residents were interested to learn that.

The *Detroit News* report had Ames claiming 1972 lot sales of $42 million and home sales of $8 million, and that Cavanagh would begin an annul $35 million construction program that summer (1973).

One editor asked Ames how he felt about advice to consumers that they not buy land without seeing it first. "Obviously I don't agree with it," Ames responded.

There were other early indications that Cavanagh and the Cape corporations had severe consumer-relations problems.

Englewood realtors tended to shun Rotonda. Even today many don't push Rotonda lot sales. "You never knew how long the operation would last," said a representative for Lee Lasbury Realtors, Inc.

There was also the constant disenchantment of the longtime Cape Haze residents. They were understandably upset when Rotonda arrived in their pristine backyard, more so when negative Rotonda publicity became nationwide and they felt besmirched by it.

"The Cape Haze people didn't want any part of Rotonda," said Dorothy Saunders Cannon. "They wouldn't even use our post office substation. They went to Placida. I know one woman who said she hated Rotonda."

Indeed, when Cavanagh arrived, Cape Haze was already a community in existence, with $50,0010 to $150,000 homes, a golf course, a cabana club and gun club, all built during the Vanderbilt era when money was real. Just as the Rotonda residents did, the Cape Haze residents formed their own Property Owners Association to protect their way of life from the unwelcome onslaught by Cavanagh's Rotonda.

They were incensed when an early Cavanagh action wiped out the old golf course they loved. Their worst fears were coming to pass. They were barely mollified when they were given free lifetime membership in the new Sunday course in Oakland Hills and rights to beachfront on Don Pedro, just like their Rotonda neighbors.

To this day, many Cape Haze dwellers still do not want to be identified with Rotonda. They are happy, even now, that Rotonda has a separate phone directory listing, that road signs are equally specific in identifying the two communities, and that the Rotonda postal district is listed as Placida instead of Cape Haze.

According to Dwight Gault, former Cape Haze POA president, "The structure of the Cape corporations was a corporate nightmare.

"This [Cape Haze] was the pearl of the Vanderbilt development," he said. "I wish I could have lived here then. Since they sold out to Cavanagh, the developer has not been nice to us . . . they've taken, never given."

A tall, distinguished gentleman, Gault came to Cape Haze in 1977, retired from a career as editor of the *Daily Digest* section of the *Congressional Record*.

He told of how upset the Cape Haze residents were when their golf course was eliminated. Even though they were given lifetime membership privileges in the Rotonda golf club, "this came back to haunt the developer," Gault said, "because it set up animosities between the communities. They used to call us the Gold Card Kids."

There were originally about 412 lots on Cape Haze, and some 200 homes. As recently as 1993, Cape Cave Corporation still owned 70 to 75 of the Cape Haze lots.

Other than the animosities between the communities, Cavanagh's other problems included a deluge of consumer litigation, including several class-action lawsuits filed throughout the 1970s, mostly by off-site lot purchasers worried about their property valuation, but also by many buyers frustrated getting their homes built and by the slow development of the community infrastructure.

Interesting enough, angry as many were, virtually all will still burble happily, "I love it here. This is heaven on earth. I wouldn't live anywhere else."

By February of 1975, the POA membership stood at 250 and would swell to 302 by year-end. It appeared to be on a solid foundation. The directors voted Tringali a three-term president. And the POA stayed right in Cavanagh's face.

In fact, Cavanagh–POA confrontations seemed certain to continue when the association nudged the Federal Trade Commission to include Rotonda in its investigation of large land developments which was then under way.

The FTC was delighted to do so. In the heavy-handed manner typical of most federal government agencies, the FTC rushed into print to justify their Rotonda probe, alleging fraudulent activities by Cavanagh.

They scared the residents to death, prompting Tringali to say, on October 10, 1975, "The FTC statements in the media were broad and confusing enough to generate fear and misconception in our community."

The POA was coming of age. Concerned at Cavanagh's bankruptcy, the association had retained legal counsel, "to help us force Cavanagh to meet its commitments," Tringali said.

They would also track the escrow account Cavanagh claimed was under Land Sales Board supervision. The account, finally unearthed in the Miami National Bank, turned out to have a balance of $6 million as of July 1975.

"Our next step," Tringali said, "was to safeguard the money and make sure it was used to produce the promised improvements."

That escrow money came largely from assessments, on top of lot prices, paid as lots were purchased. The money was supposedly earmarked for use only to build community amenities.

Tringali's own case was typical. He paid $11,062 for his lot where the assessment was $2,224. "That money was going somewhere," he said. "We weren't sure where."

Tringali was also concerned that the Bankruptcy Court, while dealing in multi-millions of dollars involving the developer and the lenders, might not consider the rights of the small property owners. Tringali didn't want the escrow fund diverted to satisfy bankruptcy matters.

There would be strident allegations later that money in the multi-millions was diverted from Rotonda development to fund Atlantic City gambling casinos and hotels. At this early stage, however, Tringali traveled to Federal District Court in New York September 10, 1975. He duly appeared before the judge and requested that the court considering the Cavanagh bankruptcy recognize the rights of the "little people." He meant the property owners, specifically the three-hundred-plus POA members.

"My trip was successful," Tringali said on his return.

During this period there had actually been some progress in building. In August 1974 the new Western Apartment complex opened on Boundary Boulevard, a thirty-unit project built by Idea Corporation. It included five buildings with six two-bedroom apartments in each.

That same month, over four thousand people visited the seven new model homes built by Sarasota's Richmond Homes. Ten months later fifty-two homes had been sold from these models, at prices ranging from $31,400 to $49,900 excluding lot.

By mid-1975 the ten-inch transmission line from the reverse osmosis water plant to the Crom storage tank in the Rotonda hub was completed. But the tank wouldn't become operable for twelve more years and stood as a symbol of much that was wrong with the Cape Cave operation.

Eleven miles of canals in Oakland Hills, Pebble Beach and Pinehurst were finished, six-feet deep and sixty-feet across; water and sewer mains were fully installed in Pebble Beach and Pinehurst; and half the roads in The Shores were now serviced with water and sewers and ready for home building.

Even though some progress was being made, two things were now obvious—Cavanagh was in trouble in Rotonda, and the POA was a going concern, nipping at the developer's heels and fighting significant battles on several fronts in behalf of its members.

During this period the recession that began with the OPEC oil embargo was fueling inflation, driving up interest rates and squeezing the money supply, inevitably altering the sensitive real estate market on which Cavanagh depended.

Also, environmentalism had caught the public fancy and become a prominent "cause," spawning a rash of energetic federal and state agencies with more and tougher environmental regulations to play with. For a land developer in Florida—a highly sensitive state environmentally—just doing business became more onerous.

Deltona

I N AUGUST 1975 Jim Petrides P.E., was formally named Cape Cave's on-site Rotonda Manager, although he had been doing the job for sometime.

As usual, rumors circulated about new ownership or developer changes at Rotonda. The most specific rumor was that Deltona Corporation was about to take over. This made sense. Cavanagh was in trouble and Deltona was a successful land and community development company, headed by the Mackle family. Their crown jewel was Marco Island.

In September, Petrides pleaded in a memo published in the *Rotonda Bulletin*: "We would appreciate it if the people circulating these rumors would refrain from doing so."

Nine months later, in May 1976, a Cavanagh news release formally announced, "Deltona Corporation has assumed management of Cape Cave Corporation's Rotonda properties."

Deltona's president, Frank E. Mackle, Jr., immediately assured Rotonda property owners that Deltona's considerable experience would be used to "help Rotonda to achieve maturity as a thriving community."

This was not a change in ownership as some had expected. Deltona came in as managers. Cavanagh still owned Rotonda. Deltona's focus was to be on construction rather than selling. They were also authorized to operate Rotonda West Utility Corporation and Cape Haze Corporation. Their assignment was to complete work on properties already sold, "Generally, to move things forward," said Bill Futterer.

The agreement between Cape Cave and Deltona was part of a structured resolution of Cavanagh's bankruptcy filing, which had not directly referred to Cape Cave, although Cape Cave's principle debts had also appeared to be in default. Cavanagh, it seemed, had been able to work a deal with the bankruptcy court, based on a plan they had submitted which was approved by their creditors. (In this plan, the extent to which the property owners' rights were considered, for which Tringali had pleaded, is misty.)

16.1 Likeable engineer Jim Petrides joined Cavanagh's Cape Cave Corporation after working for the Vanderbilt brothers. He built the "Sunday Course" in The Hills and was the on-site manager in the early years, until Deltona took over management. (Courtesy of Ethel Furia)

Cavanagh was now discharged from their Chapter 11 proceeding, was coming out from under the Vanderbilt foreclosure, and was again conducting business. Now they awaited only the FTC's finding based on its investigation.

At the time (mid-1976) 6,000 homesites had been sold and about 400 homes had been built within the 5,100-acre Rotonda West Circle. However, taking in sales in the adjacent subdivisions—Lakes, Heights, Shores, Sands, Meadows, Villas and Springs—more than 14,000 lots had been sold by the Cavanagh selling-machine.

Being smart, the first thing Deltona applied themselves to was cosmetic. They brought in Jud Johnson, who took up residence in Riverhouse and promptly announced a major beautification program. Johnson's crews cleaned up and painted everything in sight, sales buildings, the pro shop, the sewage treatment and water plants. They landscaped the median from the entrance and repaired the road into Rotonda, as far as Boundary Boulevard. They completed the Texaco service station. They restored Don Pedro Island. The residents were pleased.

Deltona also appreciated the need to neutralize the POA. Their new on-site head, Kurt Schramm (Jim Petrides had only a brief reign), met with Tringali and assured him money was readily available for development and projects would immediately be initiated.

In his final newsletter as POA president, January 22, 1977, as he was about to take office as a Charlotte County Commissioner, Joe Tringali listed these developments:

- The remaining canals, for Broadmoor, Whitemarsh, Longmeadow and Pine Valley, would be permitted, then finished. (Plans were already under review by the Department of Environmental Regulation.)
- Canal bridges in Oakland Hills, Pebble Beach and Pinehurst would be started, those in Oakland Hills that month (it was already January 22), the others in March or April. The bridges would be adequately arched to permit boat traffic. (This would become a key issue.)
- The long-awaited Oakland Hills clubhouse would be started before April 30. (However, a request that the POA see the building plans was ignored. Tringali wrote, "While we don't need a multi-million dollar clubhouse, as portrayed in Cavanagh advertising, those who tell Deltona [this] only encourage them to go as cheaply as possible.")
- Roads in Pebble Beach would at last be paved, and those in Pinehurst would follow.

- Work would begin at once on grading for the second golf course (Actually much of the layout was ready. Tringali noted that Schramm did not envision completion of the course for play in the immediate future.)

There were skeptics among the residents. Many believed that they had been lied to before. Said Ed Melton, "It didn't change anything when Deltona came in. We were made promises. They never happened."

Ray Edelstein complained about constant flooding of the existing golf course. "They started digging up and changing many of the water holes," he said. "I think they must have done something to the drainage." Seventeen years later, in 1994, flooding of The Hills golf course was a constant aggravation.

The skeptics may have been right. While Deltona, in the person of Schramm, was reassuring the POA's Tringali, it turned out that the foundations of *The Vision* were shaking.

Residents opened their *Englewood Herald* one morning to read an article reporting that Deltona officials had already approached the Florida Department of Building Regulation for permission to extend the original completion dates for much of Rotonda's development.

The implication was that property owners should prepare for massive changes in the original plan — *The Vision* — the promotion of which was what had sold so many houses and lots in Rotonda.

The revised plan would even eliminate a number of the golf courses promised. Shudder. *The Vision,* remember, promised a Shangri-La with seven golf courses, seven marinas, a commercial center with shops, a theater and a tower restaurant in the hub, and much more.

While some were less naive, *The Vision* was what many lived with. They truly believed that its wonders were what was legally committed by Cavanagh for completion by December 31, 1977. After all, they had bought property and built homes based on that *Vision.*

Learning of the changed plan, Tringali and the POA board were incensed. This was not what they had been led to believe from Schramm when Deltona came in. They saw such changes as a violation of their purchase contracts. The elimination of golf courses, for example, "drastically changes the Rotonda concept," said the POA bulletin. "We have sent a strongly worded letter to the Department of Business Regulation." They also protested the rumored changes in letters to Florida

Governor Reuben Askew, and to their representatives in Tallahassee, State Representative Fred Burrell and State Senator Warren Henderson.

Balancing the POA's irritation with the proposed changes in the development plan, the newsletter did concede that Deltona's cosmetic efforts had worked. "The entire area has been improved . . . the greens play much better," it said.

The newsletter also complimented Ed Quint, a resident and custom home builder, "who is doing a fine job building quality, good looking houses in Rotonda."

However, like comedian Rodney Dangerfield, the POA still got no respect. Tringali's last newsletter concluded, noting wistfully, that "The Rotonda manager for Deltona [Schramm] implied that we [POA] do not represent the majority of property owners . . . when of course we do."

On February 6, 1977, Tringali stepped down as president of the organization he had steered through four tumultuous years. He was succeeded by Richard Bean, with officers and directors: Charles Stockwell, Charles Kraft (his fourth term as treasurer), Catherine Toomey, Jack Labar, Julius Thomas and Tringali (as immediate past-president). Then came the real shock—the details of the plan.

In April 1977 the new Deltona plan and building schedule was fully revealed. Covering all its bases, Deltona sent the property owners a six-page letter, made a full-blown presentation to the Charlotte County Commissioners, and released details to the area media.

The letter, signed by Frank Mackle III, Deltona's executive vice-president, said the company had received "conceptual approval of a revised development proposal" from the Division of Land Sales.

The original Cavanagh schedule calling for lot completions by December 31, 1977, was extended for one year. It was noted that St. Andrews was too environmentally sensitive to even project completion dates.

The good news was that, while Cavanagh was undergoing bankruptcy, its Cape Cave subsidiary had actually negotiated new long-term loan agreements with the Rotonda lending consortium. In short, funds were readily available to complete construction and development "consistent with contractual obligations."

The bad news was found in closer scrutiny of several points in the long letter from Mackle.

While Mackle conceded the main promises in the original Rotonda design/plan (*The Vision*) he wrote, ". . . the present demand for golf facilities is satisfied by the existing course." He did, however, promise clearing, grading, and seeding of the other courses, and to maintain them as greenbelts "until population density justifies making them operational." He projected that, based on demand arising from occupied residences, a second golf course was possible by 1985. (That was eight years ahead, and it actually took twelve years, opening in 1989.)

Of greater concern was Mackle's implication that substantial cost increases faced Rotonda property owners. He stated flatly that Cape Cave's original cost projections "may have been underestimated and are not reflective of today's costs. Cape Cave will inform you of the revised assessment estimates for your particular lot in the near future," were his chilling words.

One example of inadequate cost estimates involved underground electrical distribution lines. The revised plan scrapped that idea—it would be carried through only in Oakland Hills—and "the remaining areas . . . will be served by overhead [electrical] distribution lines."

Then, piling shock upon shock, Mackle informed his readers that building on land subject to flooding—which Rotonda was—faced new county zoning regulations. These had actually been amended in 1974 and affected lot elevations, usually requiring additional landfill. "You are encouraged to consult your architect to determine the cost of the additional fill," Mackle wrote, as if everyone had an architect like they had a dentist.

Mackle then squelched once and for all any prospect of direct Gulf of Mexico access from Rotonda's canals.

"There are no plans to provide direct boat access," he wrote, noting that, "a review of the Statements of Record and Offering Statements reveals no indication of promised direct boat access."

Mackle thus dashed in a few terse sentences the lifestyle dreams of some and raised the cost concerns of many more Rotonda residents and lot owners. This was a dose of *Reality* indeed.

Mackle concluded his long letter by qualifying everything he had said. Using typical corporate legal doublespeak he noted that the FTC's 1975 complaint against Cavanagh remained unresolved. "An adverse adjudication of this matter may have a materially adverse affect on Cape Cave's ability to ultimately deliver the promised improvements," he said.

By now, Rotonda had more than 500 homes, 150 condominium units, and a population of some 1,300 according to Mackle's letter. The day after the letter was mailed, in a pitch to the Board of County Commissioners, including Tringali, Mackle claimed that Cape Cave had sold, to date, 24,637 homesites of the 34,266 platted. This was a substantial increase over the numbers cited by his father a year earlier. Many of these sales were made, it seems, in a period when Cavanagh had supposedly suspended selling activity, pending the outcome of its differences with the FTC.

Mackle told the County Commissioners essentially what he had told the property owners in his letter; but, aware of his political audience, he pitched it accordingly—stressing jobs, payroll and tax potential.

The commissioners heard that under the revised development plan, $109.7 million would be spent for building at Rotonda . . . immediate expenditures for 1977 would total $15 million, with another $14.3 million in 1978. "Nearly four hundred people will be employed," Mackle said, playing to the commissioners' concerns. "This represents an annual local payroll of $5.5 million."

Deltona's public relations approach worked like a charm. Rotonda articles broke out all over the local media. Rotonda was again "A Beehive of Activity," said the *Suncoast Gondolier* of Venice on June 20, 1977. "Less than two months after the state conceptually approved Deltona's new plan for the community, men and machines are back at work there," the paper stated.

The paper talked about a fleet of nine bulldozers, two draglines, two road graders, sixteen scrapers, twelve trucks, and four backhoes working continuously to pave roads, carve out canals and lakes, and ready future homesites as well as install utility lines in Pinehurst, Broadmoor and Long Meadow.

In July 1977, golf professional Ken Venturi, head pro at Marco Island Country Club, joined Mackle to break ground—with sand wedges—for the long-awaited clubhouse. The message from Deltona was that it would be completed by January 1978. (They missed it by only a month).

Dick Bean, having served a stormy year as POA president, resigned to be replaced temporarily by Charlie Stockwell, then, with the annual election, James Graham became the new president in January 1978.

He would be supported by Richard Tanner, William Page, Charles Kraft (again), Jack Labar, Ellis Roberts and Bob Antes.

As noted earlier, the name Antes would become significant in Rotonda historical lore.

Graham's Year

GRAHAM AND TANNER were, successively, presidents of the POA—Graham in 1978, Tanner from 1979 through 1982, another tempestuous five years in Rotonda's young life.

The first tempest during Jim Graham's era was what came to be known as "The Bridge Situation."

In early 1978 there was still no sign of bridge building, or even that it was imminent; and the non-existent bridges became a constant source of aggravation to the residents.

Three bridges that had been scheduled for completion in 1976 still allowed passage for emergency vehicles only. Two others still sported signs: CROSS AT YOUR OWN RISK.

In an effort to resolve the situation, or at least to bring it to a head, a joint meeting was planned among the POA, the Charlotte County Commission, and the developer. The problem was exacerbated when no representative of either Cape Cave Corporation or Deltona showed up.

Cavanagh's original platting agreement had included a description of the bridges. They would be forty-feet across and have a minimum of ten feet of vertical clearance between bridge and water surface. This appeared to envision small sail boats cruising the canals, as was romantically portrayed in glowing color in Cavanagh's sales brochures.

The agreement also stipulated the key locations where bridges would cross the main canal (the Rotonda River) and the major segment and finger canals in the Rotonda complex.

Finally, the aborted meeting was held. Out of it came a compromise bridge plan. The forty-foot bridges over the main canal remained in the plan, but smaller thirty-foot bridges would span the segment canals and twenty-foot bridges would replace culverts over the finger canals. There was also a likelihood that the vertical clearance would be reduced. So much for sailing into the Florida sunset.

Then, with incredible panache, Deltona made a presentation to the County Commission that deviated from the new compromise plan. It was as if the meeting never even took place. What Deltona was now after, it turned out, was a further reduction in the number and size of the bridges to fit the developer's constrained building budget. This was *Reality*.

In the view of some residents this was also too drastic. They saw it as further evidence that their lifestyle vision was fast eroding. Their rich and beautiful dream was being cheapened.

The new plan now called for twenty-foot bridges with seven feet of vertical clearance. Hardly enough to sail under. The eighteen bridges over the finger canals would now be replaced with large culverts. Several bridges that had been planned for the apex of Rotonda West (where each subdivision feeds into the hub) were to be eliminated.

Faced with a storm of protest the Commission angrily rejected the Deltona presentation, sending the company back to the drawing boards.

Meanwhile, through all the turmoil, the Rotonda social whirl continued unabated.

The Woman's Club installed nineteen new members in 1978 and now had more than one hundred members. They were preparing to celebrate the club's fifth anniversary.

The Oakland Hills clubhouse finally opened. There was a ribbon cutting by golf pro Ken Venturi. More than 400 golf club members and guests turned out to celebrate with a champagne party and cookout, following a golf tournament in which 144 golfers competed.

By now, the golf club had grown to 275 members, at $255 per family per year, plus $6 greens fees.

Home building also continued. Despite negative publicity that never seemed to let up, there was a strong demand for Rotonda housing.

Outside independent builders were now active in the community. Richmond Homes, a highly regarded Sarasota builder, opened five more new models on Pompano Street, near the entrance. The homes ranged in price from $33,295 for the Pine Hills model to $43,900 for the Lake Placid. Named after sports venues, the other models were the Belmont, Preakness and Aspen.

Other builders were also operating throughout Rotonda, including Ed Quint and Jocaro Homes. Quint built custom homes while Jocaro had seven standard home designs.

In the early summer of 1978 more clouds were roiling over Rotonda. The POA was unhappy with the progress of the FTC investigation. The organization had hoped all along that the feds would come down hard on Cavanagh, and force them to fulfill what were seen as legal commitments to the property owners. Then Cape Cave Corporation announced the formation of a Waterway Maintenance Association. This would arbitrarily impose on property owners all the costs to maintain the waterways, through assessments which the company itself would not be liable for on properties it still owned.

The POA was considering a lawsuit against the developer. First, members decided to seek state support in their confrontations with Cavanagh's Cape Cave and Deltona entities. Joe Tringali, Jim Graham, and Dick Tanner flew to Tallahassee and presented their case to the director of Florida's Division of Land Sales.

It turned out that this agency had itself filed a lawsuit against Cavanagh Communities Corporation for alleged fraud and deceit in Palm Beach Heights, a development in Palm Beach and Martin Counties, ironically, the area once planned for Rotonda East.

The state's legal action against Cavanagh is worth reviewing, because it reveals some of Cavanagh's methods of operating.

The suit named Cavanagh Communities Corporation, some of its subsidiaries, individually Joseph and Zola Klein, and longtime Klein family associate, Joel Jankowitz. These were names familiar to most early residents of Rotonda West.

The suit alleged that the developer illegally collected $2.8 million from lot-purchasers for street and drainage improvements in the 11,000-acre Palm Beach Heights. It further claimed that the lots themselves were inaccessible, with many under water, and that improvements were never made and the money was diverted.

The East Coast development had, at the time, five thousand lot owners who had paid about forty-million dollars for their property. The *Sarasota Herald-Tribune* reported that, as many of the lot owners were finishing their 1977 payments, Palm Beach Investments, a Cavanagh subsidiary, asked them to send in more money for street and drainage work.

"This was done," the paper reported, "through slick telephone and letter solicitations promising that owners could avoid future increases by paying cash up front."

Further, this was being done despite directives from the state that Cavanagh not collect a dime until street work and drainage was completed and paid for, and until other Cavanagh development funds were paid into an escrow account under court supervision.

The concerns of the POA about Cape Cave's formation of a Waterway Maintenance Association were rooted in the experiences of Cavanagh's East Coast property owners. Said one POA member, "they had been screwed, so we should have assumed we would be too. We were dealing with the same outfit."

The *Herald-Tribune* further stated that, according to state authorities, Cavanagh had collected more than $800,000 since agreeing to the escrow account plan, but had deposited only $492,000 to the account, and made no improvements. In short, $313,000 had been diverted.

State officials were quoted as alleging that Cavanagh's comptroller had sought $29,000 from the escrow account—which was in Total Bank of Miami—claiming that release of the funds had been authorized by the Division of Land Sales. It hadn't been.

State investigators complained that they couldn't trace the money. "It was passed through a chain of dummy corporations," they claimed, according to the newspaper, "that were headed by shareholders who had little or no management direction or control."

Still quoting state officials, the newspaper said, "These corporations were directed by the Kleins primarily for the benefit of themselves—to the detriment of Palm Beach Heights." The state accused the Kleins of "diversion of funds."

Another count in the state's lawsuit declared that Joseph Klein had been formally warned against selling three of his Florida subdivisions, pointing out that such sales would violate the law unless made with state approval.

Klein, according to the *Herald-Tribune*, promised to obtain the necessary approvals, but instead sold all the stock in his Palm Beach Investments to Heights Holding Company, which turned out to be owned by none other than his old pal Joel Jankowitz. Since Klein claimed that Palm Beach Heights was a subsidiary of Palm Beach Investments, Klein had, in effect, sold that development, then furnished the state with an incomplete copy of the sale and purchase agreements, said the news account.

The state cried foul, called it "sleight of hand . . . direct and willful violation of state law."

Back now to the meeting Tringali, Graham, and Tanner had with state authorities. While Rotonda West appeared to be uninvolved in this *State v. Cavanagh* legal skirmish, the POA group was deeply concerned with published accounts that revealed some of Cavanagh's operating methods.

"We had a cordial meeting [with state officials]," Graham would report to his members, "but although we were assured the utmost in cooperation, we have received little or no assistance."

The POA decided to sue on their own, and Graham issued a press release that vented all of the POA's frustrations. "Many Rotonda property owners feel they have been misled by the developers and managers of what should have been a dream community," the release opened, going on to complain about broken promises and uncompleted facilities.

The suit was filed in Charlotte County Circuit Court in June 1978, and Jim Graham said that it also resulted from the failure of either the Federal Trade Commission or the Florida Division of Land Sales "to protect the public and land purchasers as they are bound to do, from unfair and possibly illegal practices."

Graham's news release recited, in full public view, the litany of complaints and concerns about Cavanagh/Cape Cave/Deltona that Rotonda property owners had expressed throughout the eight years of Rotonda's existence: the mortgage foreclosure by the Vanderbilts, Cavanagh's bankruptcy filing, the FTC investigation, the failure to complete those elements of *The Vision* promised by December 31, 1977, and, the last straw—Cape Cave's formation of the Rotonda West Waterway Maintenance Association, an illegally formed unit that further trampled property owners' rights.

"It's a sorry history," Graham said.

A few months later Graham left the POA office and Dick Tanner was elected in 1979 as the POA's fourth president.

"Dick Tanner was a super nice guy, low key and soft spoken, a pleasure to work with," said Joe Obey.

Tanner would also have to be tough.

FTC Order

DICK TANNER'S first POA meeting, February 4, 1979, started out on a bland note, at least in terms of divisive issues or crises.

A new ambulance service was discussed. Other topics included the disposition of the Don Pedro ferry boat—which Cavanagh wanted to turn over to the POA—dredging Stump Pass, speed limits on the canals, and continuation of futile attempts to enforce the deed restrictions. Then the mud hit the fan.

It was learned that Deltona had asked the Charlotte County Planning and Zoning Board to issue a permit to build and operate an asphalt plant in the Rotonda hub.

An asphalt plant? In the hub where the restaurant and stores were to be? The residents were incensed. The POA was instructed to drum-up grass-roots-opposition to the permit.

Dick Tanner would later congratulate his members for "an impressive turnout at the hearing." However, he warned his members, "Don't relax your vigilance." He pointed out that the commissioners planned to meet on March 20 to make their final decision on the asphalt permit.

This small show of democracy-in-action was successful. On March 17, Tanner congratulated his members: "You did it. Deltona has withdrawn its application to construct an asphalt plant in the business/retail zone of Rotonda West." The commission hearing had been canceled. Everyone breathed a sigh of relief.

By June 1979, Rotonda building prices showed a degree of escalation, ranging from $39,400 to $57,900 excluding lot.

18.1 Most of the headlines of the day indicated trouble, but a few were optimistic.

Now there was also the proviso for new purchasers, "Additional fill and grade to raise the floor of the house to meet the required ten-foot elevation above a standard two-course foundation or monolithic slab will be an additional charge." In short, it now cost more to secure a house from potential flooding.

New model home names reflected "The Superstars" impact on the community: Masters, Grand Prix, Wimbledon, Squaw Valley . . . all related to sports.

In September that year, Rotonda Manor broke ground on Boundary Boulevard—three buildings, each with six two-bedroom, two-bath apartment units with balconies overlooking the tranquil Rotonda River, priced in the mid-fifties.

The Woman's Club, as usual, was active all year. The club offered dance classes among other projects, and dance teacher Marion Strunz demonstrated belly dancing with an agile group of club members. A Swedish rhythm exercise class was launched by Arlene Niess. An "Almost New" auction was held, as was a Tasting Party featuring members' favorite recipes.

18.2 Among the fun times was cross-dressing for Don Pedro Days in 1983. From left: Billie and Ed Dodds, Maddy and Herb Wood, and Whitey and Mary Newlander, before a round of golf. (Courtesy Eloise Cover)

However, there were new rumors of ownership and/or management changes for Rotonda, creating uneasiness amid the frivolity. An "interim agreement" was revealed that had Deltona managing the development for only six more months, "to allow Cavanagh and Cape Cave to develop a long-range plan," according to Frank Mackle III.

It turned out that this was preliminary to the arrival of Land Resources Corporation to take over Rotonda management. Meanwhile there was to be no construction work done during the six-month period. The residents thought, *Here we go again.*

Meanwhile, the long-awaited FTC decision had finally come down. That investigation, started in September 1975 with a fanfare of allegations of mismanagement, unfair sales practices and possible fraudulent misuse of development funds, concluded tepidly with a consent decree on January 5, 1979—a fizzle so far as the POA was concerned.

They had to listen as Joe Klein was quoted in a local paper that he had gotten off the hook. "We vehemently deny any wrongdoing but were happy to sign the consent order to avoid prolonged legal complications. We say we never did it, and the FTC says don't do it again," said Klein.

Reviewing the consent order in retrospect, Bill Futterer opined "The FTC obviously agreed that there had been misrepresentations." He pointed out that the developer henceforth had to live under the FTC order," which made selling very difficult for them."

To understand the FTC settlement, the agency's original allegations need to be stated. The principle ones were:

- Claims by Cavanagh salesmen that Rotonda lot purchases would provide significant financial return to buyers.
- Representations that the then current value of lots had substantially increased over their original sale prices. In fact, according to the Willow-Hayes Report, one-fifth-acre lots that had sold from $5,000 to $15,000 had decreased in value to $250 and $6,000.
- Promises to buy lots back from dissatisfied buyers.
- Promises that "certain recreational facilities, improvements and utilities, including golf courses and clubhouses," were planned or already completed.

- Sales pitches that indicated that General Electric Company played a major role in the planning and development of Rotonda West.
- Representations that Ed McMahon's role in Rotonda was "more than it was in fact."
- Failure to disclose that some lots were in flood hazard areas.
- Including unfair contract provisions in regard to forfeiture, property inspection and refunds.

While the Consent Agreement that culminated three years of legal wrangling between Cavanagh and government lawyers did not constitute an admission of guilt, as Joe Klein noted, it did carry the force of law with regard to future Cavanagh actions.

The decree required that Cavanagh:

- No longer represent the value, investment potential, or sales demand for its lots.
- Must initiate a "cooling off period" during which buyers could cancel purchase contracts for full refunds.
- Limit to 40 percent of the cash price the damages it could collect if a buyer breached a purchase contract.
- Extend the period for contract cancellation, contingent upon a buyer inspecting the property, to a time when the property is accessible by conventional means of transport (meaning, essentially, a car rather than a boat).
- Disclose fully all costs a buyer must pay, beyond the base lot price. (This referred to taxes and potential future assessments.)
- Disclose fully all investment information on the front page of all contracts, and in all advertising and promotional materials.
- Disclose up front that the purpose of its cocktail and dinner parties and related activities was to sell land. (This provision would protect buyers who thought Cavanagh gave parties because they were nice people.)
- Send "truth letters" to specified buyers disclosing the true facts about investment potential, Rotonda development, likely assessments and other previously hidden costs. (Such as water and sewer hookup, canal and greenbelt maintenance.)
- No longer require a buyer to join any organization where fees or assessments could be levied, unless the buyer had a voting right. (This struck at the heart of the new Waterway Maintenance Association.)

- No longer represent that seven Rotonda West subdivisions would have golf courses, clubhouses, marinas, underground power distribution, and a central core of shops, offices, a theater, and a restaurant. (In effect, stop selling *The Vision.*)

Finally, forcing Cavanagh to a workable development plan, the FTC imposed a restricted schedule of lot sales and development through June 30, 1990. Thus juggling real estate market forces, the FTC was seeking to limit the number of lots Cavanagh could sell to allow buyers to more easily sell their own lots.

In explaining its order, the FTC confirmed what Frank Mackle's letter had detailed. The agency noted that Cape Cave's original cost projections for development were too low. Owners could therefore anticipate "higher assessment charges."

The Vision was further shattered when it was declared that Cavanagh no longer planned seven golf courses, certainly not by December 31, 1977 as promised. "Areas formerly planned as golf courses will be landscaped to resemble golf courses, but will not be playable," said the FTC. However, Cavanagh was directed to keep money in escrow to open courses later, as population growth dictated.

The FTC acknowledged that property owners might have to pay $400 to $2,400 per lot to raise elevations up to four feet to comply with federal and county flood regulations.

The original plan to build a multi-million dollar clubhouse at the Oakland Hills golf course "will not now be carried through," stated the FTC. In actual fact, a $300,000 clubhouse had already been completed.

On the plus side, however, the FTC required that Cavanagh set aside a segment of Don Pedro Island's beach for use, "in perpetuity," by Rotonda and Cape Haze residents. This would include an easement to the Gulf beachfront, provision of free ferry service for seven years, after which the ferry would revert to the POA. The government's peculiar wordspeak actually referred to "a ferry or other suitable water vehicle, in good working condition."

Rotonda residents were beginning to get the point: *The Vision* was facing hard realities.

As for the POA, it was unhappy. It felt the FTC order let Cavanagh off the hook with a mere slap on the wrist, while giving no financial restitution to property buyers sucked in by *The Vision.*

In a June 1979 letter to U.S Congressman L. A. "Skip" Bafalis, the FTC explained that they had "hired an expert to analyze the financial condition of Cavanagh/Cape Cave . . . who concluded that no money was available, nor would be for years to come."

This, cried the POA, was so much smoke and mirrors. The association pointed out that while the FTC was investigating Cavanagh vis-à-vis Rotonda, the corporation "made substantial purchases in Texas, Period Bay, and other places. . . . " In short, the company was flush with cash.

Their point was bolstered by media reports of Cavanagh acquisitions in Atlantic City, which was about to become an American gambling Mecca to rival Las Vegas.

Indeed, a *Wall Street Journal* report, December 13, 1978, was headed "Cavanagh Acquires Rampart Development." The article identified Rampart as a company set to buy a casino site in Atlantic City.

Typically, Cavanagh wasn't dealing with cash here. According to the *Journal*, the company paid 800,000 of its shares for the purchase, an eight-acre site on which it planned to build a $10.5 million, 1,700-room resort hotel and casino.

The January 1979 issue of *Florida Trend* also reported the deal, " . . . Cavanagh has tentatively agreed to pay about sixteen million dollars in stock to acquire eight acres on which to build a casino and hotel of more than five hundred rooms."

Despite widespread reports of Cavanagh's business dealings in Atlantic City, FTC Counsel Jeffrey Tureck said, "There's no way we could order refunds to 22,000 people (in Rotonda). Cavanagh just doesn't have the money."

The FTC order had come down while Jim Graham was still POA president, and he had let the FTC know the frustration felt by his association's six hundred ten members, two hundred sixty of whom lived in Rotonda.

In a letter Tureck, Graham had said that his members "take serious issue with the [consent order] which relieves Cavanagh of its responsibility to meet contractual obligations."

Graham sought to have the order modified to require Cavanagh to establish an escrow account to complete the development of Rotonda, these moneys "not to be diverted to other than development." In other words, Rotonda money shouldn't wind up advancing Cavanagh's Atlantic City gambling plans.

The FTC's response was an undated, unsigned four-page letter from the FTC's Bureau of Consumer Protection. It was received by all Rotonda property owners, and did not make for cheerful reading.

"Read this letter and think about it carefully," the letter began, "then decide whether to go on making payments or stop. If you stop, you'll lose your lot and all the money you've paid so far."

Then, "to assist in your decision," the letter outlined certain facts:

- There is no resale market in Rotonda for lots that have not been developed. ("Developed" in this context meant served by paved roads and in-place sewer and water lines.)
- Substantially higher assessment charges will be necessary from many existing lot owners.
- Many lots below the one hundred-year floor level must now be raised. This will not be done by the developer. It is the responsibility of the lot owners. New houses must comply with new flood/zoning regulations.

Based on this information, the FTC advised property owners that their options were to continue making time payments, refuse to make further payments, or exchange their lots, which would likely require more money.

By now Dick Tanner had succeeded Graham as POA president, and picked up the cudgels. He told his members, in October 1979, "They [the FTC] have done us a great disservice. They have given the impression that our land is of little or no value . . . and done nothing to make the developer live up to his commitment." The FTC order, Tanner said, resulted in near panic among Rotonda property owners. However, "the order is not binding on us . . . we have the right to pursue remedy in civil court and intend to do so," he promised.

In fact, a suit had already been filed. In Keystone Kops fashion, it had bounced around during 1979 due to court problems with judges out and cases being reapportioned.

Tanner and Guy Batsel, who was now the POA's attorney, had also been to Miami and deposed officials of Cape Cave Corporation, specifically in the matter of the Waterway Maintenance Association (WMA) but also dragging in the many more general complaints that were, essentially, about the shattering of *The Vision* which Cavanagh had originally sold.

Formation of The Rotonda West Waterway Maintenance Association—forerunner of the present Rotonda West Association—had been revealed by Deltona, October 31, 1977. Deltona had created this monster without notifying property owners in advance. "We became aware of it accidentally," Tanner said. "We are adamant in our opposition to the WMA unless we have fair representation and all lots are equally represented."

WMA membership was mandatory for property owners. They would be Class A members. This sounded okay, but it turned out that only Class B members were eligible to vote and there was only one Class B member: Guess who? Cape Cave Corporation, representing all unsold lots!

These rules would apply until July 1987, or until 80 percent of Rotonda West property, 6,511 out of 8,139 platted lots, had been sold.

That's cute, said the POA, "They're imposing on us the cost of waterway maintenance through an assessment which won't apply on company-owned lots."

The costs involved included capital improvements to the canal system, purchase of maintenance equipment, and mowing and related upkeep for the canal banks and greenbelts, including those areas once envisioned as golf courses. The assessment was initially twenty dollars per lot per year, increasing 25 percent per lot per year "as necessary."

"The straw that breaks the camel's back," raged Dick Tanner, "is that they have made our payments subject to a lien on our homes and properties . . . thus placing a cloud on our titles."

And so another battle was joined, but this was one which the property owners won, for the first time.

Good-bye Cavanagh

1979 WAS A MOMENTOUS year. Soviet troops invaded Afghanistan, the Iranians seized the U.S. Embassy in Tehran, Margaret Thatcher became the first woman prime minister of Britain, and there was a "scare" at the Three Mile Island nuclear facility. And there were significant changes at Rotonda as well.

On July 1, confirming a year of rumors, Land Resources assumed the managerial functions for the community and its further development.

Land Resources was a Miami-based developer of planned communities. It had major holdings in Florida and California, including, at the time, Lehigh Acres, the well-regarded 60,000 acre, 16,000 resident community started in 1954 east of Fort Myers. (Lehigh Acres was sold in 1992 to Minnesota Power & Light Company and a Florida real estate partnership. By then it had grown to 10,500 homes and 29,000 residents, substantially larger than Rotonda.)

Jerome Cohen, CEO of Land Resources, appointed Harry Powell, Jr. to manage Rotonda, just as he had successfully managed Lehigh Acres. Powell sent in Jim Horner as his on-site manager.

Horner was a personable young man who quickly became popular around the community. He had a ready smile and a sincere attitude about the work he was doing. Moreover, unlike prior managers or developers representatives, he communicated with the residents.

Said one resident of Horner, "He was one of the nicest guys we've had here."

Fair enough. Joe Tringali hoped the new owners would meet their financial responsibilities to "buy back" lots from dissatisfied property owners, and construct the much-needed bridges. (Actually, Land Resources came in not as new owners, but in a managerial capacity. It is questionable how far their legal responsibilities went in terms of Cavanagh policies from prior years.)

While residents hoped the new group would begin making needed improvements, a Land Resources executive was quoted in the *Rotonda Review* as saying, "We are limited by the financial arrangements and the fact that we are serving only as interim manager."

He would add, "Some of the timetables set forth by the previous owners [he meant Deltona, although they were not owners, either] were unrealistic."

Powell, meanwhile, had announced the retention of two major engineering firms, from Miami and Orlando. VTN, Inc. would work on bridge development—still a sticky issue—utilities and drainage engineering. Edward Clark Engineers & Scientists, Inc. would assist with planning and environmental compliance.

Powell also promised the immediate expenditure of $1 million for road improvements.

"The County Commission has agreed to assume maintenance of roads and drainage in those areas [Oakland Hills, Pebble Beach and Pinehurst] as soon as we complete the work to their specifications," Powell said.

To which Tringali promptly responded, in his role as a Charlotte County Commissioner, "I'd be willing to accept the roads if the new owners can obtain releases from canal lot property owners to show that they are satisfied."

On the sensitive bridge issue, Powell said that work would begin January 1, 1980 on a $750,000 bridge building program. He also nailed down the specifications, which had been in heated debate—there were seven new bridges involved. Three spanned the Rotonda River and would have ten-foot clearance. The others would be seven-feet high. So much for sailing.

By spring of 1980, enough activity was obvious at Rotonda that the *Englewood Herald* took notice, saying, "While other areas in the U.S. are showing a decline in construction activity, Rotonda is experiencing a real estate boom, enabling it to confidently bill itself as 'The Community of The Eighties.' "

Indeed, Rotonda was attracting nationwide attention, the paper noted, with Harry Powell claiming completion in 1979 of "more than $2 million in residential construction," a pace he publicly predicted would double in 1980.

Powell talked about $4.5 million in condominium construction that year, and said, "We feel that being a ferry boat ride away from the Gulf of Mexico, having neat, well-kept neighborhoods, a fine golf course, super fishing and a superb location only thirty-four miles from Sarasota on the Gulf Coast are outstanding reasons for the predicted success of Rotonda."

No doubt: Powell was strongly pitching Rotonda. The residents liked that. They were proud of their corner of the world. Complain they might, but move they wouldn't.

One difference they noted from earlier management changes was the compatibility between Jim Horner and the POA.

Said Jack Labar, who would later assume the POA presidency, "They turned out to be pretty fair people. You tended to take their word when they gave it. We had some severe arguments with them at the outset, but they were nice enough guys, doing their jobs."

One of those working to keep the community beautiful was Wesley Olson, one of the earliest Rotonda residents. In 1974 Olson took a position with Cavanagh as facilities maintenance manager. He retained that position under Deltona and Land Resources, and with a staff of twelve workers concerned himself with community beautification.

"I'm proud of the community spirit of my crew," he said, in a 1980 interview with Ethel Furia. "We are doing more planting, taking greater advantage of the abundance of Florida palms."

Olson and his crew maintained hundreds of Rotonda acres spread through Cape Haze, Rotonda Shores, Oakland Hills, Pebble Beach and Pinehurst. They also kept the Community Center and administrative offices neat, clearing leaves from gutters, erasing weeds, and trimming trees and bushes.

While Olson and his crew toiled to beautify Rotonda, others were taking to the courts to vent their frustration with Cavanagh. While hundreds of individual property owners' lawsuits were settled in the corridors, one came to trial.

Punta Gorda attorney Earl Rosenthal had purchased a lot in Rotonda through his brother-in-law, a Cavanagh salesman. One day Rosenthal went to inspect his lot. According to an associate he couldn't find the lot, and at the office it couldn't even be identified.

Rosenthal's associate, attorney David Oaks, said that the Cavanagh people finally flew Rosenthal over the site, pointed down and said, "your lot is there."

So many of Rosenthal's questions went unanswered that he eventually filed suit in his own behalf. This led to another client coming in, then another, until the whole process steam rollered.

"I joined him straight from law school after I passed the Florida bar," Oaks said. "By then he was already into fifty or so cases. Thirty others came along after we went to trial in one, in 1979."

Oaks, a smallish, bearded attorney who got his B.A. from Thomas M. Cooley Law School at Michigan State in 1976, recalls that in early 1979 there were some fifty plaintiffs, from among whom Rosenthal and he selected three whose cases they felt "best illustrated fraud and misrepresentation."

The three plaintiffs were Howard Goodrich, Joseph and Mildred Gross, all of Rotonda, and Charlotta Caron of Minneapolis, Minnesota. The Goodrich suit involved four lots, two in Rotonda Springs and two in Rotonda Sands. The Caron suit covered lots in Rotonda Villas, Springs, and Sands. The Gross suit involved lots in Rotonda Springs. All the property in question was outside the Rotonda West circle.

Rosenthal and Oaks went to Charlotte County Circuit Court with a suit based on several counts, the principle ones being recision, breach of contract, and misrepresentation.

Recision is a legal concept whereby things are put back to where they would have been had there been no contract. On the back of the (property purchase) contract there was a clause that if things were not developed by a date certain, the contract was null and void, Oaks said. In which case Cavanagh would give folks back the money they had expended, and Cavanagh would get their deeds and lots back.

Breach of contract applied where due dates for certain amenities and water and sewage had come and gone, entitling people to refunds.

The misrepresentation count noted that Cavanagh prospectuses, promotional materials and sales pitches made certain promises that were never kept. The super sales pitch by Ed McMahon was also highlighted.

Rosenthal and Oaks added another count, anticipatory breach. Oaks explained this as contracts that said certain development could be expected by 1981 or 1982 (this was only 1979) but it could be anticipated that Cavanagh would breach it because they had no financial resources, no equipment on-site to do the work.

"Even if they started tomorrow, they couldn't complete it," Oaks said.

The lawsuit was tried before a six-member jury, which came back in November, 1979, with several findings: There was no fraud, because for these particular plaintiffs the date had not accrued for promised development in their lot areas. There was no misrepresentation.

As for the anticipatory breach, the plaintiffs should refile "if these things aren't done in 1982."

Judge Richard Stanley ordered judgment *against the plaintiffs* for $10,600.

Cavanagh was relieved. Harry Powell nailed down the victory and issued a warning, "where it appears that claims are not well-founded, we will vigorously defend any legal actions brought and continue to seek damages and fees from unsuccessful claimants."

At the time more than eighty lawsuits remained on the circuit court docket. All were eventually settled through negotiations.

However, in the early 1980s Rosenthal and Oaks had more than eighty potential Rotonda plaintiffs, and Oaks said, "Other law firms around town also represented handfuls of Rotonda people."

Out-of-court settlements became commonplace, mostly for individual claimants, although Rosenthal and Oaks also represented clusters of investors.

"For example," Oaks said, "We represented a group of eight or nine people out of Chicago who had invested in commercial tracts in the Rotonda core area. They had invested $90,000, $100,000, $110,000 or so," he said, "and it was clear there would be no timely development, pursuant to their contracts."

These cases were being settled, but the extent of the litigation was such that part of each settlement agreement now being pushed by Cavanagh was that the opposing attorneys would take no more of these cases.

"We were happy about that," Oaks said. "We'd had our fill." As a result of the litigation, however, Oaks believes that the Division of Land Sales toughened up their enforcement of applicable laws.

All of which turned out to be moot where Cavanagh was concerned. They were in the process of directing their business into channels other than land development. Their time at Rotonda had run out.

In June of 1980, an investment group called Rotonda Properties, Inc. acquired the entire Rotonda complex from Cavanagh. The deal also included the Cape corporations and the utility.

Rotonda Properties was headed by one J. Lawrence Eisenberg, a Miami lawyer and real estate consultant; at least Eisenberg was the nominal shareholder. The identities of other investors were not revealed, although Land Resources was said to have a $1.9 million preferred stock investment in the company, plus an option to acquire common stock.

The existing bank debt of $62 million was restructured and new borrowing capacity was allowed, with primary financing coming from Citicorp.

The residents were relieved. So far as they were concerned it was "spare me the details . . . the connection between Rotonda and Cavanagh has been severed."

They were not alone in their glee. On September 26, 1980, Joe Klein wrote his Cavanagh shareholders, "After what seemed like interminable postponements, we were finally able to conclude the sale of our primary land development subsidiary, Cape Cave Corporation, on a very satisfactory basis."

The basis was $2.2 million in cash, and free and clear title to approximately two hundred acres of beachfront property on the Gulf, which was appraised at some $8 million. What was not immediately clear to Rotondans was that the "beachfront property" was on Don Pedro Island—their island.

Klein's shareholder letter indicated that while the Rotonda property owners had been unhappy with Cavanagh, Cavanagh had been no happier with the Rotondans.

"In recent years," Klein wrote, "a substantial portion of Cavanagh's operating losses were incurred by this subsidiary [Cape Cave]." He cited 1979 revenues of $3.9 million against a net loss of $11.1 million for Cape Cave. The earlier declaration by the FTC that Cape Cave was financially unable to payback dissatisfied property owners was, obviously, because Cape Cave's funds were not co-mingled with those of the parent corporation.

Indeed, Klein's letter confirmed that while Cavanagh's investment in Rotonda had been drying up, the company had been investing heavily in the Atlantic City casino/hotel market.

That settled it for the Rotonda people. This confirmed that while their vision was falling into disarray, the sellers of *The Vision* were plowing their development money into other ventures. That these included gambling casinos made their ire that much greater.

They were also about to hear it publicly alleged that Cavanagh had "diverted" millions of Rotonda development dollars to their new Atlantic City properties, leaving the future of Rotonda marooned high and dry.

The Jackal

I N 1980 THE BIGGEST question in the U.S. was "Who shot J.R.?" In Rotonda it was, "Where's my lot and what's its value?" By now, twenty-two thousand lots had been sold throughout Rotonda, and six hundred fifty homes represented the community.

The residents worried about the tangible development they could see—or not see—outside their windows; but thousands of lot owners, mostly in the Northeast, Midwest, and Canada, were concerned about the future of their Rotonda land investments.

An answer to their prayers suddenly appeared, noisily and very publicly, in the person of Mark P. Binstein, self-appointed savior of worried lot owners. To some, Binstein gave hope that they might recover what they were now afraid they had lost by investing in Rotonda. Others viewed him as a charlatan.

One thing is true. His coming resulted in nationwide negative publicity about Rotonda and had many residents scared for Rotonda's future—their future.

Binstein identified himself as an "interstate landsales researcher." As his credentials, he cited his successes obtaining settlements for forty-five thousand lot owners in a New Mexico development, Rio Rancho, and his investigation of Great Western Cities, a development owned by the notorious Hunt brothers, Nelson and Bunker, of Texas, which he claimed led to still-pending legal actions, and many settlements.

When Binstein arrived in the Rotonda area he claimed to be representing a Chicago-based organization, The Rotonda Lot Purchasers Association (RLPA). At the request of the RLPA, he said, he had investigated Cavanagh/Rotonda. He released a sixty-three-page report of his findings which "stunned, revitalized or scared some twenty-thousand Rotonda lot owners," to quote a local newspaper.

While Binstein refused to reveal how many members the RLPA had, it was believed by some to be two thousand or more in Illinois alone. And his noisily public activities were coalescing unhappy lot owners in other states, to the detriment of Cavanagh and Rotonda.

One could access Binstein's research for $475 per deeded lot, $425 for undeeded lots, and for those who had purchased more than one lot, $100 for each additional lot.

Binstein personally canvassed the Rotonda area, held meetings in Punta Gorda, Englewood and Osprey and solicited memberships from those property owners who were seeking refunds from Cavanagh. He also announced his meetings in the local press and gave the press access, thus gaining attention.

The local bureau of the *Sarasota Herald-Tribune*, in a February 1981 article on Binstein and his Rotonda investigation, cited the case of Chicagoans John and Florence Polakowski, a couple who had been exposed to " . . . a whirlwind sales campaign that swept them into the ill-fated Rotonda development."

The Polakowskis had bought a lot, and ten years later, with $30,000 invested, they flew to Florida to find no construction on their property, and a community missing the recreational waterways, downtown business center, busy marinas, the plush clubhouse, and even bridges that would pass the county stress tests, all of which they felt they had been promised. With nothing to show for their investment, said the *Herald-Tribune*, "The Polakowskis are spoiling for action." The paper quoted Mr. Polakowski as saying, "How can they get away with this?"

To the Polakowskis and thousands of others who invested in Rotonda property, Binstein's arrival was heaven-sent.

Binstein alleged that Cavanagh, having quietly ended its plan to develop Rotonda, had then invested more than $50 million in New Jersey gambling casinos, diverting its assets and those of its Cape Cave subsidiary to and for the use of its new casino business.

He further claimed that Cavanagh had paid Land Resources $1 million per year in managing fees, "after having looted the already doomed Rotonda subdivisions of more than $8 million in cash and assets," quoting the *Herald-Tribune*.

Binstein suggested that Rotonda lots were worthless, with no market value appreciation, "because improvements planned have never been and never will be built," the *Herald-Tribune* reported.

He noted that the recently concluded FTC investigation had not compelled Cavanagh to make refunds.

The local *Englewood Herald* had Binstein alleging that Cavanagh diverted $10 million in Rotonda assets into casino businesses, acquired over $40 million in casino properties, raised another $100 million for casino/hotel construction, and paid over $4 million in "so-called" management fees to Land Resources ... all while the FTC was stating that the developer was financially unable to make refunds to disenchanted buyers.

As for the recent sale of Rotonda by Cavanagh, Binstein characterized the buyer, Rotonda Properties, Inc. as "a front company," with little or no assets.

Binstein's arrival and his charges promised "a no-holds-barred confrontation," to use his own words. Indeed, the battle lines were drawn.

A meeting was called for Punta Gorda, February 13, 1981. Almost four hundred owners and other interested persons turned up, including Richard Tanner, current president of the POA, who came to see what would transpire.

Binstein failed to show up. It turned out later that he was stuck in Cook County (Illinois) Circuit Court with about two hundred lot owners answering contempt of court charges brought by the Illinois Attorney General. It was left to Tanner to try to mollify the angry crowd, many of whom had traveled far to attend.

Another meeting was scheduled for February 19 at Lemon Bay High School and this time Binstein showed, along with three hundred fifty lot owners. He told them that their lots were worthless because Cavanagh owed Citicorp and Ford Motor Credit Company $37 million while Rotonda was only worth $37 million. "Thirty -seven minus thirty-seven is zero," Binstein is reported to have said.

According to the *Englewood Herald*, "The three-and-a-half hour meeting featured a dizzying array of financial statistics concerning Cavanagh and every company and individual involved in the [Rotonda] development." The paper said the audience seemed receptive.

The newspaper report said Binstein alleged that the recent sale of Rotonda "through a front company" was a fake, pulled off with Citicorp and Ford Motor Credit support so that repayment of their $37 million would not be in jeopardy.

The $37 million in question, Binstein claimed, was collateralized by the Rotonda lot purchasers' contracts and Land Resources was the real owner of Rotonda, and would "walk away" when it was finished milking it.

The charge was promptly refuted by Cavanagh and Land Resources. "It seems obvious what his business is," said Don Mayerson of Land Resources, adding, "this kind of publicity isn't going to help anyone."

Interestingly, Mayerson did concede to the *Sarasota Herald-Tribune* that Rotonda was neither planned nor managed well by Cavanagh, but that Land Resources was moving it towards the dream community that was originally promised. This was heady stuff.

Also responding was Joe Klein. Klein told the *Herald-Tribune* that he was contemplating a libel suit against a Naples newspaper reporting the matter. (The *Naples Daily News* had run a banner headline: Rotonda—A Case Of Land Fraud.)

Klein offered to meet with any of the twenty-one thousand lot owners and answer all their questions. He then attacked Binstein saying "This man is not an interstate land researcher. He has no connection with any state or federal agency. He makes a business out of raising the ire of lot purchasers, and it's been profitable for him."

The Cavanagh head recalled his corporation's bankruptcy in the early 1970s, claiming that there were "a full six years during which Rotonda had not been a source of income," and that "we've only been operating in Atlantic City for two years.

"Binstein is merely trying to create an aura of suspicion among lot owners so he can collect his $500 fee," Klein said.

The developer-owned *Rotonda Review* also entered the fray, warning lot owners and residents against dealing with "a person convicted of securities fraud."

The paper claimed that in 1971 Binstein had been convicted for violation of federal securities laws, fined, and placed on probation by the Federal Court in New York for "schemes and artifices to defraud lot purchasers (in another project) and misapplying funds of their association." In February, 1979, the *Review* continued, the Illinois Attorney General had alleged that Binstein " . . . specializes in organizing lawsuits against land developers."

The *Review* also tangled with POA President Tanner, claiming "Tanner associated himself with Binstein by providing Binstein with a [POA] membership mailing list and urging members to attend Binstein's February 13 meeting" in Punta Gorda.

Actually, POA newsletters at the time suggest that Tanner was ambivalent about Binstein and his crusade. Attorney Guy Batsel recalls, "I went to Washington and Dick Tanner and I had breakfast with [Binstein] . . . basically he wanted the POA to join his RLPA activities . . . and Dick Tanner, who was a very resourceful fellow, and I, concluded that his motives were entirely selfish . . . so we didn't get involved."

Tanner and Joe Tringali had, however, taken Binstein's research report to the Florida Land Sales Division and the Florida Attorney General. At the time they had not taken a position vis-à-vis Binstein himself.

Jim Horner also plunged into the battle. He gave examples of several lots in developed areas of Rotonda that had sold for considerably more than their purchase prices.

He got support from a local realtor, Harvey Pruett of Cape Haze Realty Co., who said that some Rotonda lots had environmental problems. "That's not the fault of the developer," he said, noting that many environmental regulations had changed since Rotonda lots first sold.

His firm, said Pruett, had sold homes in Rotonda ranging from $80,000 to $120,000, adding, "it's a nice place to live."

Horner said that environmentally sensitive lots were exchangeable, but acknowledged that lots not yet paid up could not be sold . . . and admitted that only about 10 percent were paid up.

A former Cavanagh salesman, Bernie Slotnik, was quoted in the *Herald-Tribune*, "All Binstein wants is to collect $500 from any suckers who will give it to him."

Mention of Mark Binstein brought a smile from attorney David Oaks. "Oh yeah, yeah. Mr. Binstein," Oaks said. "I'm not going to comment on Mr. Binstein . . . I'll just say that people were wise to seek their remedies as individuals."

On March 4, 1981, Binstein came down for another recruiting drive. On this occasion, one hundred seventy-five people attended a meeting at the Holiday Inn in Osprey, and heard an Ontario man tell of paying $15,000 for Rotonda lots now supposedly worth $28,000, only to be told "they can't find my lots."

Binstein's rejoinder was reportedly, "Maybe they'll give you a casino."

Meanwhile, the *Rotonda Review* had broadened its attack on Binstein personally, noting that an Illinois Federal Court had charged that he "illegally solicited clients for attorneys," and that he had collected more than $220,000 from lot purchasers in Indiana, Iowa, Wisconsin, Michigan, and Massachusetts.

The paper quoted Judge S. Hugh Dillon as saying that Binstein's alleged research was of little or no value. "This man," said the judge, "in the name of saving your property is ripping you off, in my opinion, and I so find."

That same day Binstein was found guilty of contempt of court in Chicago and suddenly faced a future that could include a substantial fine and a possible jail term. However, he was subsequently fined a paltry $4,500, but was enjoined from further activity with the RLPA until he signed a compliance required by the attorney general.

Undaunted, Binstein scheduled a meeting for April 7 in Punta Gorda's Memorial Auditorium. He circulated a two-part agenda.

Part One, open to the press, would cover:
- The Illinois court proceedings
- Binstein's Los Angeles meeting with Ed McMahon — his research results
- The true role of Land Resources
- Why Rotonda will never be developed as represented
- Undisclosed facts about new construction at Sands North — Developer statements alleged to be false

Part Two, closed to the press:
- Litigation plans and strategy
- Follow-up on Ed McMahon meeting
- Cavanagh's current activities in Atlantic City
- Results of meetings in California and New Jersey — Question and Answer period

Binstein invited Cavanagh and Land Resources to send representatives to refute his claims. They refused, noting in writing that the courtroom was the proper place for that.

In a letter to members of the RLPA, its secretary, one Alfred Langtry, said of Cavanagh and Land Resources, "They may use all their multi-million-dollar corporate capabilities, all their engineers and experts, all their ingenious PR . . . but they will be exposed by one man, Mr. Binstein, with but one briefcase."

On April 22, Binstein filed a $60 million damage suit against WBBH-TV in Fort Myers, the NBC affiliate station in Chicago, and the *Chicago Herald*, claiming defamation, slander and libel. He also sued the Illinois Attorney General, Tyrone Fahner, for defamation. The media stood by their news coverage, which had inferred that Binstein stirred up lot owners for the money he could get from them.

It was Fahner who characterized Binstein, quoting an Indiana judge "who called him a jackal," while conceding that Binstein had a flair for identifying problems and alerting people . . . "he seems to know where to strike."

But, Fahner said, the publicity Binstein generates "hurts people who have their property up for sale, and mitigates against further development."

By June 1981, the publicity tide had turned against Binstein, although he continued to hold meetings and pursue his allegations against Cavanagh (by now called The Royale Group) throughout the 1980s.

That month, the Florida Division of Land Sales reported that it could not substantiate Binstein's claims against Cavanagh, and Binstein's attorney, Steve Spitz of Chicago, refused to furnish documents outlining Binstein's charges. Even then, Binstein was far from finished.

By 1987 it appeared that he had induced more than six hundred Rotonda lot owners to sign onto his cause. By then, The Royale Group (formerly Cavanagh) had turned away from Atlantic City in favor of renovation of "that crumbling resort of Miami Beach." Joe Klein was no longer head of Royale.

Binstein continued to pursue settlements in behalf of lot owners, but was getting concerned that the pot was shrinking. He noted in a letter to Spitz, "$15 million in Royale net worth has vanished . . . Royale today has a negative net worth of $500,000."

He suggested that Royale's businesses never got off the ground "because of the exposure of the $120 million Rotonda swindle," and cited by name, date and detail numerous legal actions against Royale by attorneys, suppliers, banks, the FDIC, and even their own former partners, suits that were usually settled with Royale stock, a favorite Cavanagh method of operating.

"The number of outstanding Royale common shares has soared to 27 million, the market for which is virtually non-existent," Binstein wrote, apparently worried at the futility of prosecuting a company with no net worth.

His suggestions to attorney Spitz were to persuade his lot association members to settle for $2 million cash, which he believed Royale could borrow, plus 10 million Royale shares, worth about $1 million at the time.

He would then proceed against Joe Klein personally in court, seeking a cash judgment, and against Ed McMahon for $1.5 million. He claimed McMahon had already offered to settle for $500,000.

Binstein was still in the news in 1991. In September that year, an article by Trevor Armbrister appeared in the prestigious *Reader's Digest* which characterized Binstein as "mesmerizing," and said he had held more than three hundred meetings in seventeen states and Canada, raking in $2.5 million in the process.

Armbrister traced Binstein's wide ranging activities, using Ralph and Connie Paone in his Rotonda segment. Seems the Paones had moved to Florida in 1976, planning to build on property they had bought at Rotonda. "To their horror," the article went, "they discovered their lot was in a flood zone where nobody was allowed to build."

Cavanagh spurned their pleas for help, so in 1981 they wrote Binstein a check for $475 and joined the RLPA "with some 1,500 others."

They were told, wrote Armbrister, that Ed McMahon was being pressured by Binstein to testify against the company, and the members were therefore sure to recover their losses.

Over several years the Paones got reports from Binstein citing "progress," until it became clear that McMahon wouldn't testify. They were then told that McMahon would be the target of their litigation, and "because he has deep pockets," they would still recover. All it would take was another $75 for "expenses" and there would be results in eight weeks.

The Paones heard no more. According to Armbrister's article, Binstein didn't respond to their letters or return their phone calls. "We got duped," said an angry Connie Paone.

The article concluded by citing the case of one Rotonda defendant who had agreed to a pretrial settlement of $300,000. "Binstein, his attorneys and expenses took every penny. The victims received nothing."

Water, Water, Everywhere

THE NEGATIVE PUBLICITY that resulted from Binstein's allegations against Cavanagh upset the Charlotte County Commission. They were concerned about the possible effect on a request filed July 9, 1980, by Rotonda West Utilities for a 400 percent increase in water and sewer service rates. It was in the county political pipeline being considered by the County's Water and Sewer Advisory Board.

The residents were up in arms at the prospect of the rate increase, which would affect 823 water and 679 sewer customers in Rotonda West alone.

Ed Hennessey, who would be president of the POA seven years later, still claims: "The developer was always trying to get their construction costs out of the water consumers."

Hennessey, former superintendent of Public Works for Geneva, New York, said, "I was familiar with what you should get and for how much."

In the battle that ensued in public, the utility cited cumulative losses of $1 million since its inception, based on an investment in the system of more than $11 million. The company noted that a $50,000 county tax increase had itself amounted to 53 percent of the utility's revenue. Chemical and labor costs had also increased.

The residents got a letter from Ed Shapiro, vice-president of the utility which declared, bluntly, "The utility simply cannot continue to provide service . . . at either the [old] rate or at the rate suggested by the [county] committee."

POA president Dick Tanner weighed in, pointing out that "the requested rate increase could result in bills as high as $100 per month."

Tanner used the issue to promote POA membership . . . "So that we can present a united front."

Even Joe Tringali was disturbed. From his position as a County Commissioner he told his colleagues," These rates will make Rotonda West a very exclusive community . . . few people could afford to live there,"

To help it to respond, the County Commission sought recommendations from an independent rate consultant and from its own Water and Sewer Advisory Committee.

While all this was going on it was rumored that the county was inclined to grant an increase in the range of 150 to 200 percent. However, while awaiting data on which to base their final decision, the commission granted the utility an interim increase of 50 percent, pending a public hearing February 4, 1981, at the Community Center. The utility flatly rejected the 50 percent interim increase.

By then their billing was already arbitrarily reflecting the full 400 percent increase that they had requested. Their rationale was that the county had taken more than sixty days to consider their original request.

Hennessey recalls the flap the rate increase caused, when monthly water/sewer bills normally around eleven dollars soared without warning to forty dollars. Some residents claimed to be paying increases of as much as 700 hundred percent. They were appalled.

By March the commission had rejected the 400 percent increase, but approved whatever rates would assure the utility a 13.5 percent profit, or $28,600 a year. The excess the utility had been charging while the new rates were pondered was to be refunded to utility customers, plus 10 percent penalty interest.

The utility promptly appealed the increase as too low, asked for a stay of the directive to make refunds, and then claimed their appraisal, at $5.5 million, was too high by $4 million. They said this was part of the reason the rate hike was needed in the first case.

The utility's position was rejected on April 9. Attorney John Hathaway, representing Property Appraiser Oliver Lowe, said the utility company had failed to contest the appraisal in the time allotted by law.

On April 29, the utility withdrew its water-rate lawsuit and agreed to pay the refunds as directed, to 860 customers. By May they had refunded more than $100,000, and things had cooled down.

Meanwhile, on April 22, William Henry Vanderbilt had passed away at seventy-nine, at his home in Williamstown, Massachusetts. The *Englewood Herald's* obituary noted Vanderbilt's ties to Rotonda.

"The Vanderbilts developed the Rotonda subdivision," said the paper. "After they moved to Englewood, William and Alfred Vanderbilt raised [Santa Gertrudis] cattle on their 2-V ranch. They sold the property when it was zoned as developable, making the economics of cattle raising difficult."

Vanderbilt's death recalls the importance he attached to water. A valuable commodity in Florida, it was important to life and to the running of his ranch. Needing potable water the Vanderbilts had sunk wells pretty much where they chose and started the Cape Haze Water Company to serve their community.

Then Cavanagh came along. The company knew the utility was inadequate for the needs of a community as large as Rotonda. So, in 1971, in one of their smarter moves, they had constructed a reverse-osmosis water-treatment plant—at a cost of $560,000.

Osmosis is a natural process which causes a chemical in solution to pass through a semi-permeable membrane from an area of high concentration to an area of low concentration until the concentration is equal on each side of the membrane. The size of the spaces between the molecules that make up the membrane control which chemical molecules are able to pass through. Those larger than the spaces obviously can't pass. A reverse-osmosis water operation applies four hundred pounds of pressure to raw water with a high saline content, forcing the water molecules through the membrane and leaving the salt behind, along with most of the remaining undisolved material. Larger particles of undisolved contaminants are usually removed by filtration prior to the water undergoing reverse osmosis.

Water in the Gulf of Mexico has a salt content of some 35 thousand parts salt to one million parts water, but the hydrostatic forces pushing it through sand and rock formations to Rotonda and the mixing with fresh groundwater cleans it to a concentration of about 10 percent of that. Two deep wells supply the R.O. plant. These go down 154 to 164 feet, at which level all they draw is brackish water pushed in by the Gulf.

The plant was initially rated at 500 thousand gallons a day, and currently (1994) treats about 400 thousand gallons daily. For every 1 million gallons of untreated water, the plant can produce 500 thousand gallons of potable water. The residual saline concentrate is discharged, under tight regulations, into the West branch of Coral Creek.

At the time, the Rotonda operation was billed as "The World's Largest Reverse Osmosis Plant" and employed what was then a revolutionary concept in water treatment. The plant was on Cape Haze Drive in Rotonda Shores, near what used to be the Texaco service station and a small delicatessen.

According to the *Englewood Herald* (January 20, 1971) "the costs expected to be carried by Cape Haze Water Co. include $352,000 for plant, $100,000 for grading and paving, $50,000 for equipment and pumps, and $21,000 for the huge reservoir."

21.1 Built in 1972 by Crom Manufacturing Company, the 5 million-gallon reservoir tank in the hub of the development remained inoperable until the late eighties.

The R.O. plant works in conjunction with the reservoir, the long familiar green tank—recently painted tan—that anchors the hub of Rotonda. The tank was built in 1972 at a cost of $296,000 by Crom Corporation of Gainesville, Florida. Made of pre-stressed concrete, the tank is 180 feet in diameter, 43 feet high, and has a potable water storage capacity of 5 million gallons.

It was the R.O. plant in particular that attracted George Manyak to Rotonda. "I knew fresh water was a concern in Florida," he said. "I was impressed by their excellent R.O. plant."

At the time Cavanagh crowed, "Only St. Petersburg has as large a tank." Cavanagh's boast was premature. The events that would, in time, drive them from Rotonda also diverted them from putting the Crom reservoir into operation. Built with great fanfare, when it was finished it remained unconnected and inoperable until the late 1980s. There it stood, for years, a symbolic white elephant—in this case, green elephant—irritating lot owners and residents alike.

"The revolving restaurant was supposed to be on top of it," says Ed Hennessey.

Hennessey appears to be correct, recalling a statement by the developer, "The central location [of the tank] was the most practical and economical site . . . because it would in no way interfere with the permanent structure that will ultimately be built above and around it."

Today, the Cape Haze wellfield on Boundary Boulevard has a daily capacity of 300,000 to 500,000 gallons. This well water goes through a lime softening plant and is supplemented by some thirty wells located in a star pattern around the Crom tank whose water is treated by aeration, filtration and chlorination.

By 1992, the average water consumption through the utility operation was 402,000 gallons. There were more than 2,282 water meter connections, seventy-seven of which were for commercial or multi-residential customers. The utility is permitted to make annual withdrawals of 1.66 million gallons of water a day.

A 1992 engineering study by Englewood's Giffels-Webster Engineers, Inc. says Rotonda gets its water from three aquifer systems. These are the surficial acquifer (down to one hundred feet), the intermediate aquifer (from one hundred to six hundred feet) and the Floridian aquifer (deeper than six hundred feet).

The sewer operation in Rotonda West operates through eleven miles of mains laid alongside the eleven miles of water main in each part of the community's pie. The system operates at 625 thousand gallons a day capacity, and already has a permit to expand that to 1.2 million gallons.

It serves more than two thousand customers, and operates either by low pressure pumping or gravity. The low pressure method is aerobic, with air providing much of the cleansing process. This is the system used in The Lakes, Windward, The Villas and The Heights. The remainder of the community utilizes the gravity system where the sewage falls downgrade in the mains to a pumping station from which it is pumped to the treatment plant.

That's how it is today, but the new management that came to Rotonda in 1986 was horrified at the water/sewer system they inherited.

The Rotonda Environment

J UDY WYSOCKI, field investigator for the Department of Natural Resources (DNR), paints a disturbing picture of a hurricane's potential for devastation in a local populace blissfully unconcerned about it.

Wysocki points out that "the whole Rotonda area is [in] a flood zone."

A direct hurricane hit on the Gulf Coast between Fort Myers and Sarasota would undoubtedly cause the destruction of much of Rotonda. The storm surge itself would likely dissipate about 4,000 feet inland, but water levels would rise dramatically in Charlotte Harbor, the Myakka River, Coral Creek, Buck Creek, and most of Rotonda's otherwise benign canal system.

Beyond the water threat, any reasonable hurricane would have "Rotonda roofs flying all over Charlotte County," according to Rolland Geiger, a Rotonda resident whose wry observation came before his attorney cut off further comment (he was in litigation with developer management at the time). He has credibility, however, having been a building inspector up north, prior to coming here.

Now consider this. On the world map, Florida is halfway between the Tropic of Cancer and the 30th parallel, north latitude. Travel around the world from Rotonda on that line, and you'll pass through Algeria, Libya, Egypt, Saudi Arabia, Karachi in southern Pakistan, Allahabad in India, northern Burma, Foochow in China, Central Mexico, and the lower Baja Peninsula. Hot, dry places all, many with more sand than even our renowned Florida fairway bunker (sixteenth hole, The Hills).

To that extent, then, Florida's climate is explainable. Add its extremely low elevation to its latitudinal fix, and the environmental sensitivity of the Cape Haze Peninsula is clear.

Many of the federal and state regulations that impact Rotonda's development came into being after Rotonda was well along. Suddenly, in mid-stream, Cavanagh faced new and tricky environmental aspects that were not in evidence when they brought their grandiose plans west.

The adaptation of their plans to this barrier island coastline were exacerbated by the formation, in 1975, of the Department of Environmental Regulation. Then later developers had to contend with the Henderson Wetland Act, passed in the early eighties, which put greater focus on Charlotte Harbor, which flanks Cape Haze, site of Rotonda.

Says Judy Wysocki, "Rotonda property was affected to the extent that it impacted Charlotte Harbor, which some of the creeks do."

As Wysocki pointed out, before the late 1960s, land developers did pretty much what they chose. Other than the loose monitoring of developers' sales methods by the state Division of Land Sales, their main environmental concern was the benign attitude of the U.S. Army Corps of Engineers which, back then, was not looking at things from an environmental viewpoint.

In the beginning, the environmental impact on Cavanagh would obliterate large portions of their original development plan, particularly as applied to The Springs, The Meadows, The Villas, Sands South, The Shores, and, inside the circle, St. Andrews. These areas became impossible to develop as originally planned because of new state and federal regulations governing wetlands.

One persistent problem was that Cavanagh's enthusiastic sales machine had already racked up thousands of lot sales in these subdivisions.

The two main issues are control of the runoff of chemicals and nutrients into waterways that feed Charlotte Harbor, which is the usual result of unfettered population expansion, and protection of the wetland swamps, bogs, marshes and uplands that are habitat for scrub jays, eagles, plovers, bobcats, white pelicans, and other endangered or threatened wildlife, and support crucial plants and unique biological systems.

In January 1984, Buell and Lissa Webster of Rotonda led a group from the Venice Audubon Society on a Rotonda tour. A newspaper report claims that they sighted seventy-nine species of birds, including many rare ones.

The Rotonda area is also home to a number of bald eagles, America's national bird. They are frequently spotted from the golf courses. They were listed as endangered in 1969, just as Rotonda West was launched. During development, work was delayed for seven months on one of the Buck Creek bridges by the discovery of an eagle's aerie near the bridge. Recently, because of the efforts of conservationists throughout the country the eagle has been taken off the endangered list.

Great Blue Herons are a majestic sight at Rotonda. They stand over four-feet-tall and have a six-foot wingspan, and gracefully stalk around and feed in the waterways. Other common animal sights are egrets of all kinds, blue-winged teals, and wood storks, an endangered species of wading bird. Also wild hogs, armadillos, bobcats, and seven classes of turtles.

The endangered Florida panthers, which some residents claim to have sighted around Rotonda, are reportedly down to fewer than fifty individuals statewide. Indigo snakes, also seen, are on the list, too. Gopher tortoises are rated a species of special concern, and scrub jays are a threatened species.

The renowned environmentalist, Marjory Stoneman Douglas, wrote of a Florida where "fabled and familiar beasts moved [once upon a time]," referring to various mastodons and other mammals that once made this area home.

One famous holdover from eons past is familiar to all Rotonda residents—the alligators that sun themselves by most of the golf course ponds. In 1982 one resident found an alligator in his swimming pool; another had her kitchen invaded by an alligator. Golfers frequently surrender their stray balls to such adversaries, taking a safe drop elsewhere.

Rotondan Harry Virtue recalls the early days when "we caught blue crabs in the salt-water canals and wide-mouth bass in the fresh-water ponds."

The late Ray Young, who moved to Rotonda from Cincinnati with his wife, Dorothy, in 1977, would set crab traps every week in the salt-water canals around Rotonda. Dottie would steam Ray's catch and they and their friends would enjoy a scrumptious, if messy, feast. These were some of the pluses.

But environmental concerns certainly impacted Rotonda's development. In 1971, a Cavanagh ad promoting Rotonda West in *Florida Trend* magazine referred to "conservation" indicating that the developer was conscious of environmental concerns even before the regulations tightened. The advertisement promised, "we value our natural mangroves . . . plan to set aside thousands of acres . . . for wildlife preserves."

17.1 The social whirl included Sadie Hawkins Day. Dorothy Young was one participant, as Mammy Yokum. Dot came to Rotonda in 1976 with her husband the late Ray Young. (Photo courtesy Dorothy Young)

In 1977, Deltona's Frank Mackle III alerted Rotonda property owners " . . . some platted areas [of Rotonda] contain wetland vegetation." This, Mackle warned, made it doubtful that the required development permits would be easily obtained. He promised a lot exchange program, even suspension of installment payments, until the environmental regulations were clarified.

As late as 1986, with the advent of James Penzell's management of Rotonda Properties, environmental issues were more evident than ever.

Penzell's marketing executive, Bill Futterer, said that one of his first tasks upon arriving at Rotonda was "to move about a thousand lot purchasers in The Springs, and another thousand in The Sands, where new regulations made development unfeasible."

Futterer stressed the need to protect particularly eagles, gopher turtles and scrub jays "as now required by law." He said, "Right now [early 1994] discussions are in progress with regulatory authorities about scrub jay protection in Windward, particularly around the golf course. In 1969, nobody worried about scrub jays."

July Wysocki said it best. "Before 1969, environmental concerns were voiced by people seen as radical bunny-huggers and tree-huggers. There were few laws or regulations in effect."

But after that, Cavanagh's *Vision* would meet environmental *Reality*.

The Antes Agreement

THE DEVELOPMENT OF Rotonda was a bonanza for lawyers, most of whom nested around the Charlotte County courthouse in Punta Gorda. With the advent of the new Rotonda community, many quickly established branch offices in nearby Englewood and Grove City.

Among them were Wotitzky & Wotitzky, and Guy Batsel. Batsel had worked in Wotitzky's office for a number of years until he struck out on his own. As Rotonda grew and western Charlotte County became more developed, he first opened an office in Englewood, then later moved to Grove City to handle his many Rotonda clients. One of these was the POA.

Among the hundreds of lawsuits filed involving Rotonda, few were of earth-shaking consequence, except of course, to the plaintiffs. Most were settled out of court, usually after interminable delays that kept the plaintiffs thoroughly frustrated. The basis for most lawsuits was that *The Vision,* which helped to sell many Rotonda lots, had not come to pass as originally presented.

One early case eventually turned out to be significant. It had been filed by the Wotitzky firm and was handled by W. Cort Frohlich, assisted by Guy Batsel, when both were still with the Wotitzky firm.

The suit was a class action against Cape Cave Corporation. The plaintiffs of record were Robert T. and Diane Antes, George and Hilda Kantner, and Richard and Barbara Tanner. All were Rotonda property owners and POA members.

Cape Cave was represented by Richard M. Goldstein of the Miami law firm Goldstein & Tanen.

Bob Antes, an unassuming, gentlemanly ex-marine, came to Rotonda in 1977, after twenty-seven years in Canton, Ohio and seven years in Williamsport, Pennsylvania, working with Prudential Insurance. After he took up residence Antes became active in the Rotonda community. He was on the building-fund committee of the Community Church and joined the POA.

Antes and his wife owned two Rotonda lots at the time. They had paid $5,400 each for the lots in 1970, a total of $16,540 in deferred payment terms. One lot was in Whitemarsh, one in Long Meadow. They subsequently exchanged these lots for two in Pinehurst, costing a total of $17,078 in deferred payments.

When they joined the class action against Cape Cave, Bob Antes says, "We really didn't know much about it. I was approached as being available and suitable for depositions. I guess I was the type they needed, I just went with the flow . . . and my name was alphabetically at the top of the list."

Many of the complaints in the action focused on the developer's failure to live up to his promises and agreements, as had hundreds of other lawsuits. Among these were Cape Cave's failure to enforce the deed restrictions, a constant canker in the community.

However, this suit also named as a defendant the Rotonda West Waterway Maintenance Association. It is believed that the high-handed creation of an RWWMA, with its unchecked power to assess lot owners and threaten their property ownership actually triggered the flood of litigation.

The complaint referred to language in the lot purchase agreements which said, in effect, that the developer would maintain the waterway and drainage system. Lot purchasers would pay and be assessed for part of the cost.

The formula called for a cost to purchasers of two cents per square foot of each lot, or approximately two hundred dollars for the average ten thousand-square-foot lot, to offset construction costs; then, additionally, maintenance support costs of four dollars per lot per year.

The legal complaint alleged that the way Cape Cave formed, in October 1977 (through its then management company, Deltona) a Waterway Maintenance Association, gave the association—and thus the developer—the power to levy special assessments for capital improvements, and authorized them to hold plaintiffs personally liable for annual charges, interest, and costs of collecting funds, under threat of a lien against their property.

It further noted that it gave the RWWMA (meaning the developer) complete voting control until December 31, 1983.

The suit stressed that the RWWMA was not formally established as a drainage district, but could levy annual charges of twenty dollars per lot, effective January 1979, and increase that 25 percent annually if they chose.

The lawsuit was settled August 1, 1983, in Charlotte County Circuit Court. The detailed provisions of the settlement came to be known as The Antes Agreement, and thus enshrined the name Antes forever in Rotonda's stormy history.

The parties to the agreement were the plaintiffs, Cape Cave Corporation, the Rotonda West Property Owners Association and the Florida Land Sales Division. Cape Cave was directed by the court to pay plaintiffs' legal fees, up to fifty thousand dollars.

"The main thing the Antes Agreement did was return control of the Rotonda West Waterway Maintenance Association to the property owners, represented by the POA, and to establish the discipline of a timetable and methodology for certain improvements to occur," said Kendall Leach. Leach is responsible for the day-to-day operation of today's Rotonda West Association (RWA) which has evolved from the RWWMA.

Today, Rotonda still functions under the requirements of the Antes Agreement, and the developer—whoever that they may be—must meet its specific provisions, as enunciated by the court.

Among these were:
• The RWWMA was continued in existence under Cape Cave's control, but for not less than four nor more than seven years (August 1990). During this period the POA must be represented on the RWWMA board. (The POA assigned then President Ed Hennessey to that task.)
• Cape Cave was required, within that seven years, to complete the canal system and maintain the canals. The developer's obligation in this was to begin, in each subdivision, when residences were built on 25 percent of the lots.

- After four years, control of the RWWMA was to be relinquished to the POA before the end of the seventh year. At that point, the POA was to elect all but one member of the RWWMA board. The remaining board member would represent the developer.
- The newly structured RWWMA would have authority to levy charges, fees or special assessments as required for the continued maintenance of canals and greenbelts.
- Cape Cave was ordered by the court to give the POA all its pertinent records, as well as $2,500 towards furnishing an appropriate office.
- Cape Cave was ordered to pay levies and assessments on all their developed but still unsold lots.

In addition, the Antes Agreement required the developer to carry through a range of improvements, and to establish new Investment Trust Agreements (ITAs) to pay for them. They were also to draft an outline of material change orders.

The material change orders were to set down schedules and costs for improvements which the court said must be carried out. The ITAs were, essentially, escrow funds to insure that the money was available for the work to be done. The ITAs were to be set up in the National Bank in Miami, and invested in certificates of deposit. All ITA withdrawals required the advance approval of the Division of Florida Land Sales.

What all this did, as Ken Leach noted, was bring some discipline into the development process and establish regular maintenance of the canals and common areas, all of which was beyond the capabilities of individual property owners.

Said Leach as late as May 1994, "It's a settlement we all have to live with." Indeed, copies of the Antes Agreements are kept readily to hand in the RWA and POA offices, for quick reference.

In immediate terms, the Antes Agreement directed the bank to disburse some $7 million then in escrow. Then, $178 thousand was to go into ITA No. 2 for use expressly for golf course and marina construction. That sum was the amount Cape Cave had estimated was necessary to complete one golf course and one marina.

In fact, at that time, Cape Cave was estimating the cost to build six golf courses and marinas at from $1 million to $1.7 million—if they built within six years. The difference in the figures reflects up to six years of potential inflation.

It was clearly spelled out in the Antes Agreement that the golf courses were to have equipment sheds, proper sodding for fairways and greens, sand for traps, fertilizer and pest control. The marinas were to have eighteen docking spaces.

Then, $418 thousand was to be dispersed to Cape Cave for any improvements completed prior to the Antes Agreement. The balance of the money was to go into ITA No. 1, to be used to complete the improvements in Rotonda West. However, while the agreement applied specifically to Rotonda West—inside the circle—$5,426,000 could be withdrawn from ITA No. 1 for labor, materials and engineering services in any Rotonda subdivision.

Cape Cave Corporation was also required to file annual reports with state authorities. These would set forth work done and moneys expended. The developer was thus to be closely monitored from then on, and the residents had a voice in the RWWMA.

Painting the developer into an even deeper corner, the state was authorized to force him to deposit up to 17 percent of all payments received on his Rotonda West receivables, if it determined that an ITA account held less than was required for particular work.

Finally, a $2,500 "improvement charge" was tacked onto lot sale prices, to be payable by lot purchasers in one hundred monthly payments of twenty-five dollars each, beginning one year after they bought their lot. These moneys would be deposited in the ITA account.

How did the POA react to all this?

After a brief period of self-congratulation, the organization realized that, sooner or later, perhaps without much warning, responsibility for canal and common area maintenance would fall on the property owners. Cape Cave could give ninety days notice, then transfer the responsibility.

After mulling over the significance of this, the POA board decided, finally, in the late 1980s, that it wanted nothing to do with such a responsibility. It was believed that the best solution was to turn the task over to Charlotte County.

This meant establishing a Municipal Service Taxing Unit (MSTU) to fund the maintenance. To the board's way of thinking, 7,500 lots at ten dollars per lot per year would do it, generating $75 thousand a year.

They polled the residents and lot owners as to their opinions.

At first, the idea got strong support, although the MSTU was an unknown to most of them.

Ken Leach recalls being on the POA board when John Meadows was president. "John and I, and Robert Underwood, met often with the county . . . to find out exactly what we must do to set up an MSTU." Underwood, by November 1990, was working for Rotonda Properties Inc., helping to manage Rotonda.

"The more we checked into it," Leach said, "the more it sounded like the county was a costly way to go."

Vince Carvalho, a resident who later became POA president, said, "Many of us filled out the cards supporting the MSTU, but we didn't have any data about ad valorem costs."

Carvalho clarified the matter in a letter to the owners of improved property. He noted that the taxable value of Rotonda West property was then over $108 million, according to the county appraiser. A single property with a taxable value of $50 thousand would pay $250 under an MSTU, versus $60 under the cost per lot method.

He further pointed out that under an MSTU the land would have to be deeded to the county, stripping lot owners of control. Moreover, he wrote, greenbelt maintenance would be a function separate from canal maintenance, at additional cost. And the county fee for administering an MSTU ran about 25 percent of the budget, which at the time was $500 thousand.

Finally, under an MSTU, lots owned by the developer would have their maintenance support payments reduced from sixty dollars to only eighteen dollars.

Armed with all this new information, the property owners asked themselves: "What are we doing to ourselves?" They began to object to the MSTU idea.

Unfortunately, in February 1990, the POA had gone ahead and formally requested of county authorities the formation of an MSTU, at that point supported by five hundred of their unenlightened members. The County Commissioners had already published notice of a hearing on the matter.

Now, John Meadows, POA president, tried to get the issue removed from the commission agenda. "Not possible," said County Administrator Tom Frame, "It can't be arbitrarily withdrawn." However, the commissioners could vote it out.

In the final analysis, the Commission voted the MSTU in place, meaning that to this day it is on the county taxrolls, but, in effect, is in limbo unless or until a formal request is made to activate it by a majority of the RWA's voting membership.

Since all this flurry, canals and public areas in Rotonda West were maintained by the RWWMA, under developer control, until October 1991, when the RWWMA became the Rotonda West Association (RWA), in which membership is mandatory for Rotonda West property owners (unlike the POA, in which membership is voluntary).

However, the transfer from developer to lot owner control was itself fraught with argument.

The Battle for Don Pedro

I N T H E E A R L Y 1980s, Rotondans had finally relaxed—happy to be rid of Cavanagh at last. To be sure, there were never ending aggravations as the community continued to grow. But with Cavanagh gone, a corner seemed to have been turned. Until, unexpectedly, new rumors began to spread that Don Pedro Island was still in Cavanagh's clutches, and, horror upon horror, was about to be developed.

In the early selling of *The Vision* of Rotonda West, Don Pedro Island was the crown jewel. It is an ecologically sensitive barrier island between Knight Island to the north and Little Gasparilla Island to the south. It sits southwest of the Rotonda circle, just beyond Cape Haze.

The beautiful island, with its miles of white, sandy beach facing the Gulf of Mexico to the west and the protected Intracoastal waterway to the east, was a spectacular element of the original *Vision* Cavanagh sold so aggressively.

Cavanagh's Commercial Generating Principle, the document that outlined their schedules and development plans, called for Don Pedro to have, by December 1972, a docking area on the island's east side, a two thousand-square-foot pavilion with refreshment serving capability, restrooms, changing rooms, locker facilities, walkways from the docks to the beach on the west side of the island, all landscaped.

Don Pedro, the developer had said, was "for the residents of Rotonda . . . and . . . persons brought to Rotonda as prospective purchasers of land or structures."

It was reasoned that after a Cavanagh cocktail party and picnic party on Don Pedro, few would resist contracting for a lot in a community with such an idyllic attraction.

Needless to say, the original Cape Haze residents weren't thrilled with Cavanagh's Don Pedro parties. "It really burned them," Helen Waldron said, recalling, "the parties Cavanagh threw on Don Pedro, complete with band . . . you could hear them quite clearly across the water . . . all the screaming and hollering from that pavilion."

But Rotondans loved their island. John Meadows, who would become president of the POA as it headed into the nineties, remembers, "We'd go to Don Pedro, all our friends went, and we took our company from up north. That was a wonderful period . . . but it was also another thing that came to a screeching halt, another headache for the POA when Cavanagh threatened to develop."

There had been early warnings that Cavanagh planned to build on Don Pedro. They were spelled out in the company's 1971 annual report: "During 1971, the company developed a tentative land plan . . . and when completed, the island community will have both beaches and boating within a short walking distance of its apartment buildings, each of which will be separated from the others by greenbelts of lush tropical foliage."

Other early warnings of Don Pedro's eventual development—with several luxury condominiums, no less—were evident in the company's promotional materials.

But the likelihood of building on Don Pedro was overlooked by most Rotondans in the euphoria that went with having their private island in the Gulf of Mexico to play on, and to which they had legal access in perpetuity. They set about enjoying their island.

Don Pedro Days became a traditional annual event, with Rotonda's social organizations sponsoring special activities.

One year, for example, the Round Town Garden Club held a flower show, the Woman's Club had an Arts and Crafts Fair, crowds visited the community center where the Fiesta Club's "Old-Fashioned Ice Cream Social" was in full swing, and the Coast Guard Auxiliary conducted demonstrations of safe boating techniques at the Oakland Hills Marina. The American Legion held a "Meet-Your-Neighbor" social, and two hundred-sixteen golfers competed in the Don Pedro Days Golf Tournament, followed by a buffet luncheon, complete with free beer and the music of Les Elgin's eighteen-piece band.

But the highlight, as always, was on Don Pedro's beach, where a family-oriented sea-and-sand party featured games, contests, treasure hunts, sand sculpture events, kite flying, and an egg toss.

By 1973, Cavanagh had caught up with their Don Pedro development timetable. A refreshment stand was opened, offering hot dogs, ice cream bars, cookies and soft drinks seven days a week, from 11 A.M. to 3.30 P.M.

Cavanagh began to have frequent parties and picnics on the island for prospective buyers. From all accounts no expense was spared.

The developer also ran free ferry service on the *Roundabout*, a pontoon boat which also took Rotondans on Intracoastal Waterway cruises. The boat, powered by twin outboards, operated daily on a fixed schedule from Gasparilla Marina in nearby Placida, under Captain Arthur ("Hap") Lassen.

Lassen became well liked in the community. He was a colorful character who had been a cowboy and a commercial fisherman and was full of stories. He lived on Little Gasparilla, Don Pedro's island neighbor to the south.

The ferry was popular. Lassen ferried thousands of passengers between the mainland and Don Pedro from 1972 until 1980. In 1981 the ferry was renamed *Capt. Hap* in Lassen's memory.

Cavanagh's *Bulletin* crowed, "Cavanagh has developed this beautiful beach facility for you . . . they want you to enjoy it . . . all the Don Pedro facilities are there for the Rotonda residents," and also noted that lifeguards were on duty every day. In the early 1970s these were usually resident volunteers Michelle Manyak, Marcille Ballard, Cheryl Connolley, and Gerry Lynn Schriedel.

By 1979, Cavanagh had completed a new dock at Don Pedro, christened it "The Port of Don Pedro," and again publicized "our enchanting recreational spot and its white sand beaches."

Harry Virtue said, "We had a lot of beautiful times at Don Pedro all through the seventies." Indeed, virtually all Rotonda families spent happy hours there. It was part of the lifestyle.

In 1979 Rotondans, while disappointed with the bland outcome of the FTC investigation of Cavanagh, had nevertheless been overjoyed by one part of the FTC ruling—where a four-hundred-foot waterfronted beach area was formally designated for use by Rotonda residents, in perpetuity, with assured access and free ferry service to be provided by the developer until 1983, when the boat would be turned over to the POA.

It was not immediately noticed that the FTC order included the phrase, "While there are no current plans for development [on Don Pedro] it may eventually be developed with condominiums and other high rise structures." Shades of Miami Beach in all its aluminum and glass tackiness.

And so the good times eroded. It seemed that there were always problems, constant confrontations, never-ending litigation. Rotondans who had breathed a sigh of relief when, in 1980, Cavanagh severed its relationship with the community and sold out lock, stock and barrel, now faced the awful reality that Cavanagh still owned their island and planned to build on it.

24.1 The pristine beach at Don Pedro Island, just offshore from Rotonda, was considered their private preserve by early residents who banded together to fight the threat that it might be developed with condominiums. (Courtesy of Leonard and Olga Durham)

When it finally dawned that Cavanagh's sale of Rotonda had not included Don Pedro, and that Joe Klein himself still owned it and seemed intent on developing it, or selling it for development, there was a new issue for the POA to rally round.

POA founder and still County Commissioner Joe Tringali was again roped into Rotonda service. Events show that, as usual, Tringali performed valiantly for his community.

Tringali began by writing the deputy assistant director of the FTC, Congressman L. A. ("Skip") Bafalis, and a U.S. senator named Lawton Chiles. In turn, Bafalis and Chiles wrote to the chairman of the FTC, Michael Pertschuk, and the POA initiated its own grass-roots writing campaign, furnishing its members with suggested text.

And thus the battle for Don Pedro was joined.

The essence of Tringali's letter barrage was that Cavanagh was already skirting the intent of the FTC consent order. While they did provide a beach area, as required, it was on the remote northern part of the island, "far removed from the beach area used by the residents for the past nine years, and from the docks and other facilities," Tringali wrote.

The politicians all responded politely, but not helpfully. The FTC said that the recorded easement complied with the commission's order, which had not provided for a specific location on Don Pedro.

Congressman Bafalis, who represented Florida's tenth district, responded to Tringali, "The Rotonda West situation has been a source of great frustration for me ever since coming to the Congress, and I know it has been equally disheartening to the property owners." This politic concern didn't solve much.

The most serious matter to the Rotonda residents was the potential development on Don Pedro of high-rise condominiums.

According to Jack Labar, POA president for 1983, 1984, and 1985, "There weren't any disappointments [at Rotonda] so far as we were concerned. I mean, I came here with my eyes open, and we worked, so we were occupied every day, not just playing golf."

However, Labar recalled, "We did get into a class-action suit regarding Don Pedro . . . we discovered the island was in fact mortgaged . . . Cavanagh's chairman, Joe Klein, simply wrote himself a mortgage without going through his own board of directors."

Labar said that the POA retained a Sarasota law firm, Nelson & Smith, which successfully had the title to Don Pedro frozen, making Klein's mortgage "pretty useless," Labar said, adding, "Banks don't care for mortgages that don't return anything."

This brought things to a head. The POA didn't want title to the island, Labar said, "so we decided the best thing was to get the state to buy it."

The concept had a certain brilliance to it, because it appealed to federal and state authorities based on their relatively new concerns about the environment. The practice of government acquiring sensitive land to save it from development was just then coming into vogue.

Joe Obey said, "Don Pedro was a strong selling point down here, so we moved to get the state to take it over, with continuing rights to us and the Cape Haze people."

24.2 Treasure hunts and parties on Don Pedro Island were constant during the early days of Rotonda. In the unlikely event of rain, the pavilion was a welcome shelter.

Actually, the Cape Haze residents had their own separate beach, adjacent to Rotonda's Beach, on the Gulf side of the island. Rotonda also had a beach on the bay side. The beaches were joined by a forty-foot strip of pathway. The Cape Haze group at first fought their own battle for Don Pedro, through the Cape Haze Property Owners Association. But eventually the POA and CHPOA joined forces in the matter.

Enter Tringali again, who gets most of the credit for the success of the idea of Don Pedro secure as state land. While Labar said, "I honestly don't know if they [Cavanagh] planned to develop the island or not. . . . Joe Tringali had no doubts about it."

Tringali himself recalls that Cavanagh made a request for some zoning action, which he caught as County Commissioner. "Their plan was for a massive residential development," he said.

He pointed out that there were zoning restrictions, one unit on ten acres of environmentally sensitive land, "but they planned to get around that in some fashion, with condo units."

Tringali's concern was valid. It recalled an earlier report by Elizabeth Whitney in the *St. Petersburg Times*. Whitney wrote that when Rotonda East was disapproved as a residential development, Joe Klein had filed a "declaration of condominium" in Martin County.

"This fabulous condominium city-in-the-round had no timetable for development . . . [and] . . . all improvements were to be assessed against the buyers," Whitney wrote. The buyers, however, got no vote in the condo management until the last unit was sold. And the developer himself would own one unit, thus giving him absolute control.

According to Whitney, "[this] permitted the developer to nullify the condominium at any point . . . without the vote or joinder or consent or authorization or approval whatever of any other persons."

The point was that the company, through this tactic, could circumvent county, state and federal requirements via the condominium vehicle, sell the land as a condominium and then dissolve the condominium when it was still raw land—without notifying anyone. Whitney quoted a real estate lawyer, "It would shock the conscience of a court."

Worry about such possible Cavanagh tactics now entered into the battle for Don Pedro.

Tringali was also concerned that Cavanagh might be able to grandfather its Don Pedro building, "because state and federal regulations were still in the early stages of formation."

The solution? Lobby the state to buy the island and turn it into a state park. The state had recently initiated the Save Our Coasts program. There was also a Conservation and Recreational Lands program. State authorities surely would be receptive.

Meanwhile, a group of residents had also acted in the matter, using a different tactic—another class-action lawsuit against Cavanagh. Plaintiffs included the Burris, Hennessey, Doran, Labar and Ray families, and Jean B. Bennett. They alleged that Cavanagh was welching on its published guarantee that Don Pedro was reserved as Rotonda's "private island," although that never had been the extent of the commitment. A section of beach, yes. The whole island, no.

Jack Labar, POA president, said in his newsletter, "If we want to keep what is rightfully ours on Don Pedro, we will have to fight for it." He warned that the opposition "seems determined to push us out of the way."

The lawsuit was settled out of court in December 1984.

Meanwhile, elements of the state government were also focused on Don Pedro, as was the press.

Judy Wysocki, who would join the Department of Natural Resources as a field inspector in February 1985, had previously been an activist with the Environmental Confederation of Southwest Florida (ECOSWF) and its president. Wysocki remembers the battle for Don Pedro beginning with what she calls "Shed Gate." When the federal Coastal Barrier Resources Act (COBRA) was passed, Wysocki declared, workshops were held across the country, wherever there were barrier islands, to identify the most sensitive and get them under COBRA protection.

This, supposedly, would discourage development on these islands. After all, they were not only environmentally sensitive but potentially dangerous to life and property in the advent of heavy weather, particularly the hurricanes that annually threaten Florida's coastline.

Under COBRA, such islands were denied federal flood insurance, thus averting possibly heavy insurance costs to the taxpayer.

However, existing structures on these islands would be grandfathered, so the logical question became, what constitutes a "structure?" The answer given at the Fort Myers workshop: two hundred-fifty-square-feet with a roof, a door and a window.

That did it. When this information leaked, the rush was on to get "structures" erected before COBRA was formally enacted. Charlotte County authorities then exacerbated the situation by issuing accessory building permits for Don Pedro in violation of their own zoning code.

Federal and state field agents immediately swung into action. They flew over and photographed the islands. Says Wysocki: "When the feds saw photos of all these sheds it hit the fan." National focus on the matter followed a widely syndicated Jack Anderson column in which he christened the scam "Shed Gate."

By then Wysocki and her group were following a path parallel to Tringali and the Rotonda and Cape Haze POAs, lobbying at both federal and state levels every agency and committee that might support government purchase of Don Pedro to prevent its development.

Wysocki used the damage from the June 1982 No Name Storm to support the issue, forwarding island damage photos to the appropriate authorities, along with clean-up cost estimates. The clear implication was that the cost to taxpayers would be enormous if Don Pedro and other islands, including Knight Island, were developed.

Another tactic in the battle was to get the coastal construction control line moved inland. Seaward of this line, regulations impose more stringent engineering and construction standards.

Wysocki's group—noting through photos that the No Name Storm created severe damage on Don Pedro—suggested relocating the control line inland.

This was done, ultimately, but during the 180-day period before it all became official, developers were on Knight Island driving pilings and building twenty-four-hours-a-day, seven days-a-week, right up until the deadline, in an obvious attempt to become grandfathered. The result, according to Wysocki, was about three hundred dwelling units on the north end of Knight Island that she believes should never have been permitted.

By this time, however, Klein had become a willing seller of Don Pedro, most likely nudged by Great American Bank of Dade County, which held his mortgage with the island as collateral. A warranty deed record shows that Klein sold Don Pedro to his own company, Cavanagh Communities.

Finally, in December 1984, purchase of 129 acres of Don Pedro Island by the state of Florida, under the Save Our Coasts program, was approved. The cost, a little over $6 million. The island would always be available to Rotonda and Cape Haze residents . . . and the rest of the public as well. It was now a state park.

The next and final step that involved the POA was disposition of the Don Pedro ferry. Cape Cave Corporation had been required to maintain free ferry service until May 1986, then turn it over "in good operating condition" to the POA.

After thinking about it, the POA decided it could not afford to operate the ferry, maintain it and house it at a marina. The forty-foot, tri-hulled craft cost $40 thousand a year to operate. Insurance was a major item. With state ownership of Don Pedro, a new ferry permit was required. And, it was noted, the POA was a voluntary membership organization. Not all Rotonda property owners belonged, so some might benefit without paying their share.

These matters occupied the POA for the next several years.

May 1986, marked the legal end of the developer's responsibility for the ferry. Cape Cave was ready to turn it over to the POA.

However, in December 1986, the *Sarasota Herald-Tribune* was noting, "Physically, the ferry that used to run between Rotonda and Don Pedro Island hasn't moved an inch since May."

The next effort was to try to get the state to accept it. After all, Tringali pointed out, without the ferry the DNR had a state park on Don Pedro nobody could get to.

But the state didn't want to be in the ferry business either.

Said Ed Hennessey, "You wouldn't believe the hassle over that boat . . . do you know it was originally delivered to Cavanagh COD? Does that tell you something?"

As late as March, 1989, the *Charlotte Sun Herald-News* was still on the case. The paper weighed in with an editorial: "County Should Get Ferry Going."

The paper said, "Don Pedro Island has a magnificent public beach . . . but you can't get there from here."

The solution, said the paper, was for the state to acquire the ferry from the POA and operate it in the public interest . . . even with a four dollar round-trip passenger fee. No thanks, said the state.

Said John Meadows, "We beat our brains out trying to figure out where to store it, how to fix it, whether to fix it, and to find some way to continue to operate it to get people over to the island . . . it took us several months to even get title to the damn thing."

Today, Don Pedro remains its pristine self, available to visitors with boats, or by a privately operated ferry originating at the Ship's Lantern restaurant opposite Fiddler's Green. The round-trip costs five dollars and fifty cents.

To that extent, the Rotonda residents won the battle for Don Pedro, and most probably don't even know it.

Dry Your Laundry Indoors, Please

I N 1974, WHEN Jack Labar came to Rotonda, it wasn't to retire. He started Labar's Pool Service and then Lemon Bay Hardware. Both businesses are well established today. Labar didn't know that ten years later he would be a community leader, serve a three-term stint as POA president (succeeding Dick Tanner) and would become mired in the contentious and frustrating issue of deed-restriction enforcement.

To this day, many Rotonda property owners seem blithely unaware that their property deed carries certain specific restrictions on their use of their property, although entering Rotonda on Boulevard West takes you past a large sign that says, "ROTONDA WEST—A DEED RESTRICTED COMMUNITY," as if it were an aphorism.

Indeed, the original developer had sold Rotonda that way, having a concise list of restrictions filed December 29, 1969, with the Charlotte County Circuit Court. But the developer shrugged off enforcing the restrictions, so they were updated and reissued March 28, 1984, during Labar's POA tenure, and in November 1985, Labar sent out a clarification of the restrictions, in the wake of the Antes Agreement.

Essentially, there were restrictions on building walls or fences, or unauthorized "structures or buildings" on lots, including boat docks. Vacant lots had to be kept free of trash. In driveways: no tents, travel trailers, cargo trailers, motor homes or recreational vehicles including boats and boat trailers, except under certain conditions. (Time was allowed, for example, for loading and unloading.) There would be no unauthorized signs.

There were more. The actual document of Rotonda's deed restrictions is long, detailed and complex in its legalese. But the major aggravations usually focused on overnight, or even lengthier parking of RVs in driveways.

Cavanagh's original intent seems reasonably motivated. The first subdivision, Oakland Hills, had no electric pylons or overhead wires. It had curbed streets. Unsightly fences were banned. And, without trucks, vans, recreational vehicles, boats or trailers parked in driveways, it looked neat and appealing.

If that concept had been carried through the entire Rotonda development, the deed restrictions would surely have enhanced property values by upgrading the community's appearance.

Unhappily, curbed streets and underground power proved too costly. Both ideas were abandoned after Oakland Hills. Moreover, the enforcement of the deed restrictions suffered from the developer's inaction.

Ed Hennessey was POA vice-president under Labar. "We inaugurated enforcement," Hennessey said. "What was going on . . . or not going on . . . was a farce. There were fifty-five or so violations and nothing was being done, but the developer didn't want to get involved."

By 1987 Hennessey was POA president. The matter of deed restrictions was an irritant to him. He found it difficult to get the names of violators from title records. Lack of legal clout didn't help—the POA represented only a fraction of the property owners.

However, during Hennessey's term the POA began to take people to court for the more flagrant violations. Mostly, these concerned unauthorized vehicle parking in residential driveways or vacant lots.

Said Hennessey, "Altogether it wasn't a very popular thing. I mean, one of the ministers was one of the worst violators and his flock protected him. When I asked them to speak to him about it, they wouldn't. Finally we took him to court. We won, but it took a year and a half to do it and we weren't very popular."

In fact, they took several cases to court, proving their serious intent, and most violators would settle when they found the courts liable to impose day-to-day fines for as long as violations continued.

One resident, Jerry Ullrich, was chairman of the POA's deed restrictions committee and active in the organization into the early nineties. Ullrich was described as "a tiger on deed restrictions."

Ullrich credits Hennessey with sparking the enforcement issue. He still considers it "mind boggling" that Cape Cave Corporation would ignore the enforcement of deed restrictions, "because their very purpose was surely to make things attractive to help sell the area."

Meanwhile, for years, those who wanted the restrictions firmly enforced were frustrated by the inaction. On the other hand, those who parked their boats, trailers or RVs in their yards, when confronted by their irate neighbors who regarded these vehicles as a blight on the community, usually suggested, not always politely, what could be done with the deed restrictions.

With the advent of the Antes Agreement, the matter came to a head. The agreement directed the developer to "strictly and vigorously enforce deed restrictions, with special emphasis on those related to campers and motor homes."

The developer was also made to pay 50 percent of the costs to prosecute enforcement cases, up to five thousand dollars per year.

To relieve what was a contentious community issue, the agreement forced the developer to designate an area suitable for parking RVs, boats, trailers, campers, trucks and vans.

The original area designated was on Boundary Boulevard, across from the gazebo on Rotonda River and the Oakland Hills clubhouse entrance. It was about an acre in size, and quickly became an eyesore to people leaving the clubhouse. They could look across, beyond the gazebo, and see a panorama of motor homes. One resident recalls trying to assure a visiting guest that Rotonda wasn't a trailer park.

In time, the matter became academic. The lot was too small. The POA negotiated with Cape Cave Corporation for three acres in the hub, then had it lighted and surrounded with a security fence. An RV Association was formed and a sixty dollar annual fee was established.

Kendall Leach remembers the negotiations. "They [Cape Cave] agreed to level the area and make it ready, but we had to handle the lighting, security fencing, and financial aspects of it." That's why the RV Association was formed.

These moves resolved the most contentious of the deed restrictions issues. There are still complaints about unkempt vacant lots, but they are quickly handled.

Ray Edelstein notes, however, that drying laundry outdoors assaults the visual senses of many residents. "There was a house down from me where the woman always hung her laundry out to dry," Edelstein said.

"I went to ask Ethel Furia about it, and together we looked, but there was nothing [in the deed restrictions] that said you couldn't hang laundry outside."

To this day, to the annoyance of many residents, particularly golfers, laundry of various unsightly garments can frequently been seen flapping in the breeze, a scene that one described as "more like downtown Calcutta."

Fore

ROTONDA, OF COURSE, is a golf community. One of Cavanagh's major selling points about Rotonda was the unique idea of seven golf courses, named for the days of the week. To play a different course each day would appeal to most golfers.

When Cavanagh launched Rotonda West, an early part of their plan was to phase out and then eliminate the existing nine-hole Cape Haze course. This, as much as anything, upset Cape Haze dwellers who already felt their splendid isolation was ruined by Rotonda's arrival. They had loved their golf course and its special place in their hitherto pleasantly quiet lives.

But Cavanagh plowed ahead. The Sunday Course (now The Hills) was built during 1971 under the direction of Jim Petrides. It opened November that year, just as the first ten families began to move in.

According to George Manyak the course was "absolutely gorgeous," and most agree.

The original Sunday Course was "beautiful," said Chicagoan Ed Melton. "In terms of its layout it was a good challenge." Melton remembers that dues then were two hundred thirty-five dollars, plus five dollars more if a cart was used.

The first pro was Walter ("Red") Lathrop, a popular figure who, with his much beloved wife, Eunice, got Rotonda golf started. As George Manyak recalled, "We had about fifty members in the early years and many of them had never played golf." This didn't bother Lathrop, who worked cheerfully with them all, while Eunice played with the women.

Bill Hyde also recalls these as happy days. When he came home from college, Hyde said, Jim Petrides and Wes Olson would give him work around the project. Hyde was able to play a lot of golf then, and did so frequently with Red Lathrop, "almost every afternoon."

Hyde also remembers the course being "in great shape." He, with Petrides and Lathrop, played the first official round on The Hills.

"Silvio Furia and I and several others set up the first Men's Golf Association," said George Manyak. Although Manyak continued to work after coming to Rotonda from Ohio, he was an enthusiastic golfer. "There were a bunch of local businessmen and contractors, about twenty-five or thirty, who used to play the Sunday Course every Saturday."

Manyak was elected first president of the Men's Golf Association in May 1973. Milo Hall was vice-president, and Silvio Furia secretary/ treasurer. Manyak won the inaugural tournament with a low net 67, on June 16, 1973.

Early accounts suggest that the women upstaged the men, forming the Woman's Golf Association in 1971 with twenty-four women, ten of whom played only nine holes. Donna Spadaforra was the first president, supported by officers Lillian Cottingham, Flora Perrin, and Mary Von Glahn. Helen Waldron became president in 1972. Most of the group were Cape Haze residents.

Rosemary Toops remembers, "We had our first invitational with the women from Wildflower. Having no clubhouse yet, I had them all to our house, which was quite a chore and had me uptight for days."

In an appropriate social vein, on November 20, 1973, thirty women gathered for a blind-partners, better-ball match. It was won by Dot Christianson and Judy Whitesell with a net 64. Nine hole winners were Nettie Bean and Lova Zeigler with 32.

"Next week," intoned Ethel Furia's *Bulletin*, "Ladies Day will feature a Cat Fight . . . with bonus points for eagles, birdies, pars."

In fact, by 1973, Ethel Furia's *Bulletin* was keeping the entire community alerted to all activities, and generally listed golf events and winners, including the club championships, which then had Men, Women and Junior classifications.

One early *Bulletin* reports that the first resident golf champions were Don Ziegler, twelve-year-old Joe Furia, and Yolanda Manyak. A local newspaper account indicates that they got their trophies in 1972, at the community's first anniversary event, a dinner in Punta Gorda.

Unfortunately, official records were not kept during the early years and champions were not formally "posted," probably because there was nowhere to post them. Only the faltering and often conflicting memories of several residents give us the champions' names: Bill Duke, Carl Rupp for three years, attorney Scott Ittershagen, Richie Whitesell, Joe Cornelia, and Hank Thode a couple of times. Ed Melton thinks he won the championship "somewhere along the way," in 1973 or 1974.

In more recent times, Gene Parvin and Bill Van Allan both won three times, and Dick Yust, Bill Wingo (1993) and Tom Holcombe (1994).

On the women's side, Rosemary Toops, an avid golfer, said "That's all I wanted to do when I came here." She remembers that there were sixteen participants in the first Women's Golf Association. It would grow to almost two hundred.

Helen Waldron was the first officially recognized women's champion. She won in 1973 with a 7 & 5 victory over Shirley Petrides, and repeated through 1978. Betty Jane Dorsey won in 1979, then Pat Stottsberry ran a seven-year string into the mid-eighties. Jan Davison won in 1993 followed in 1994 by Lemon Bay High student and team member, Heather Gripe. The course itself was "a good track," as some have opined. However, after but a year in operation, holes in one had been recorded by David Kilborn (the first), Ralph Horton, Sil Furia, Hannelore Knoeckel, and assistant pro Bob Burke. Burke had become Lathrop's assistant in 1972. Of the group, only Furia was a Rotonda resident member, the others coming from Cape Haze.

By 1974 there were two hundred or so men golfers. Twenty-seven showed up at the Men's Association meetings. As for planned golf, Ray Edelstein recalls, "we'd all go to the first tee and hang around until there were four guys. They'd tee off, then the next four as they arrived, and so on. It was pretty informal."

The "clubhouse" at the time was best described as a "shack," although the early members remember it fondly because of the "good times" they had there. It was on the spot now occupied by the cart shed.

Helen Waldron chimes in, "They had to shovel sand away from the door in the mornings, to get it open. They'd torn out all the trees, flattened whole areas to build, and sand flew everywhere. It was sad . . . wonderful big oaks . . . terrible."

Nonetheless, "We had a ball," said Ed Melton. "There wasn't a nicer course. Friday night was party night, after Guys & Dolls. Everyone took part."

Ray Edelstein: "The women would bring a coffeepot and we'd put twenty-five cents in for coffee. It was our club then and we ran it like a club should be run, for the members. Great fun."

In 1974, Cavanagh was promising a proper clubhouse "in the near future," publishing an architect's conception in one of their brochures.

"I remember it," Waldron laughs, "it looked like something out of *Arabian Nights* . . . with sauna, health club, a parking garage underneath and valet parking. I had to laugh, and I thought: that'll be the day."

26.1 The clubhouse from the *Arabian Nights* as originally designed, with a health club and underground parking, before common sense took over.

John Meadows also remembers the original clubhouse plan. "We didn't exactly have the clientele for it," he said. "We're not $200,000-home people. They got a bit fancy."

In 1977 Jack Bileaux came in as head golf pro, assisted by Cary Tate. A new junior golf clinic for ages six to sixteen was started under Tate's tutelage. But the head-pro position tended to be a revolving door in these days, until, in 1979, Ray LaGoy took over.

LaGoy was an interesting individual, whose name comes up quickly when the early golfers recall the "old days" at Rotonda. He was from Lake Placid, New York, and owned Whispering Oak Golf Club in Lima,

Ohio. An experienced golf pro, LaGoy was a twenty-nine-year Class A member of the PGA, a former sectional officer for the PGA and Ohio's Pro of the Year.

LaGoy's appearance at Rotonda seems, to a degree, to have confirmed Rotonda's credibility as a golf center. He and Wanda had three children, and theirs was a golf family. Above all else LaGoy was a golf teacher, and his focus was always on the members and their concerns. LaGoy made golf at Rotonda memorable, by all accounts.

26.2 Ray LaGoy, respected as Rotonda's golf professional, beloved as a human being.

"Club activities revolved around Ray," said Pat Stottsberry. "Since he left, it's become less fun and more of a business."

Ed Melton agrees, describing LaGoy as "A super guy. Everyone loved him. He could name every person who came to the course . . . their kid's names, where they were from, their handicaps. He was one of the funniest guys you ever met, telling stories for hours and having everyone roaring."

John Meadows: "LaGoy related to the members on a very personal level."

Mike Balistierri, who came to Rotonda in 1977 from Milwaukee, brought with him his annual Cardiac Capers Golf Tournament, which he had initiated up North. "I just mentioned it to LaGoy and we were off and running," he said.

Balistierri told how the tournament he started in Milwaukee raised seventy-two dollars its first year, then four thousand dollars, then six thousand dollars in succeeding years, improving each time.

"Since we've had it at Rotonda we've donated over forty thousand dollars to the Englewood Hospital Auxiliary," Balistierri said, with justifiable pride. The money purchased and operates two courtesy vans to transport patients, and lifeline units, fifty-three of which were connecting patients to the hospital twenty-four hours a day in 1993. Cardiac Capers is now an annual tradition.

Eventually, after years of fanfare, the new clubhouse was completed in February 1978. It was "much toned down" from the "Taj Mahal they originally planned," the members agree.

So, with a brand new clubhouse, an excellent course and a popular pro, Rotonda golf should have been on the road to success and contentment.

Not so. There was still much grumbling about "the six other courses they promised us." Litigation was ongoing, constantly being publicized to the detriment of Rotonda's reputation.

Ed Hennessey, a self-admitted golf nut, said that he came to Rotonda because "There were to be seven golf courses, all in place before 1980." It never happened, not even two, far less seven.

Even the developer was unhappy. By 1981, Land Resources Manager Jim Horner was complaining, "The Oakland Hills Country Club has been operating at a loss for years."

Horner said Cape Cave " . . . invested over $1 million in land and improvements, but lost $70,000 in both 1979 and 1980, and by now over $200,000.

"To continue to operate in the face of such losses Cape Cave must now move into a sales posture," Horner said, resorting to corporate-speak. "If the company doesn't succeed," he warned, "all these services and facilities will cease to exist."

This was a dash of cold water. However, most residents just went on about their business, enjoying life. LaGoy would report that more than two hundred rounds of golf were being played daily, and projected that "1981 will be our best season ever, thanks to the membership."

Membership itself was at an all-time high, LaGoy said. He ticked off the wide range of golf events under way. The club championship was in progress, a match play event with six flights that ran for five weeks, a true test for the eventual champions.

Jan White, clubhouse manager, opened the dining room to the public for breakfast and luncheon. Dinner was being served only on Wednesdays and Fridays. The clubhouse was also expanded to include a screened lanai.

1986 was a significant year in Rotonda's history. In January, Ray LaGoy left. The golf community was stunned. It seemed that an era had ended.

Personable young Bob Ridge came in as head pro. He had been a pro for six years, an assistant at Ohio's Bowling Green Country Club, then head at Riverby Hills.

By now, resident memberships were $675 for single and $750 for dual memberships. Non-residents paid $800 single and $1,200 dual. But Ridge's tenure would be brief.

The fifth Rotonda management group had arrived.

The Fifth Developer

1986 WAS A momentous year. The space shuttle Challenger exploded as millions watched in horror. A meltdown at Chernobyl fanned world concerns about nuclear power. In the Philippines, a woman named Aquino came to power, succeeding her assassinated husband.

At Rotonda, the fifth developer management assumed control in the person of James Penzell.

In 1980, after Rotonda Properties, Inc. had acquired the Rotonda companies from Cavanagh Communities Corporation, it had conveyed the shareholder assets to Land Resources Corporation. Land Resources, its subsidiary Lehigh Corporation, and Rotonda Management, Inc. had continued to manage Rotonda.

At the time, giant Citibank had become the lead lender and there had been an infusion of $37 million in new financing.

But by 1985, the Rotonda companies had a negative net worth of about $26 million and were in default on their loans. One local business report said the Rotonda companies lost $9.4 million and $12 million successively in 1984 and 1985.

That was enough for Citicorp, Citibank's parent. With foreclosure in serious prospect, Citicorp turned to one of its consultants, James Penzell, and asked him to rescue the community, and their money.

Penzell arrived in 1986 as president of Rotonda Properties, Inc. He immediately restructured Rotonda's debt, formed a new management team, and began to try to restore the residents' morale, which was at a low point.

Penzell had been an architect, contractor and developer for thirty years. Since 1974 he had specialized in real estate asset restructuring.

As a consultant to First National City Bank (subsequently Citicorp) Penzell had worked to restructure the bank's real estate pool, which included numerous development companies, some similar to Rotonda.

In fact, when Citicorp tapped him Penzell was working to restructure a residential development built around Raintree Golf & Country Club in Charlotte, North Carolina.

"Penzell seemed a pretty nice individual," said Joe Obey. "His arrival was the best thing to happen to Rotonda since the beginning, although he didn't reveal much about the structure behind his organization."

The residents' curiosity about the new management, especially those who had to work with it, was not unreasonable, given the sometimes traumatic history of their community. However, most were content to know that one man was now in charge, and that he had a plan.

That he had a plan, indeed, quickly became evident. It envisioned Rotonda substantially different from the splendiferous one suggested by the original *Vision*. It was based more on the late 1980s economy and reasonable projections of the nineties.

It was, however, reassuringly progressive in that it resumed the selling of Rotonda and continued community development. There were even hints that new golf courses were in prospect. This alone was enough to cheer most of the residents, whose visions of the seven courses promised had collapsed to the reality of one: Oakland Hills.

The marketing of Rotonda would fall to William Futterer, brought in by Penzell in July 1986. Futterer was a native of Rockingham, North Carolina and got into marketing in the Charlotte, North Carolina area after college. He had worked with Penzell at Raintree.

Penzell and Futterer began by analyzing the task facing them at Rotonda, and it turned out to be a daunting one.

Penzell said that after they came in, "it required about two years just to sort out the pieces. It was like buying a Rube Goldberg machine and receiving it in a crate in pieces, without assembly instructions and with some of the pieces missing.

"We found the sales of lots appeared to have been completely random. They were all over the place, about eighteen thousand of them, with no visible plan."

Penzell said the disarray that he inherited included a lack of basic bookkeeping or records, and many infractions of federal, state and county laws. Some, he said, were significant, including failure to follow the requirements of the 1979 FTC order, and, in some instances, even outright tampering with it. There were also violations of Florida's Land Sales Agency regulations.

"It was pretty obvious," Penzell said flatly, "the original developer never intended to develop the property."

Some of the lots that had been sold, the new management found, were in the eastern and southern sections of Rotonda, in areas declared undevelopable for environmental reasons even before they had been improved.

27.1 Aerial view of Rotonda facing west northwest toward Don Pedro Island. Platted areas in the foreground are The Meadows and Sands North, separated by CR 771 and, to the right, The Lakes. (Courtesy of Cape Haze Realty Co.)

Said Futterer, "There was a need to completely revamp sales and marketing."

They began this by temporarily halting all international and interstate sales of Rotonda land, and all retail installment sales. They formed a construction organization, and started a new community development program.

To the satisfaction of residents who were conscious of the changes, Penzell's basic objective seemed to be to treat Rotonda as a community in development, rather than a land-sales business, and to build amenities to support housing.

But also, "We had to implode the company down to a manageable size," Penzell said.

Penzell and Futterer began a massive program to exchange, for some 3,500 lot owners, undevelopable lots for developed ones. The exchange program was difficult. People came to inspect their current property, found they couldn't sell it in its undeveloped state, and, says Futterer, "We had a lot of angry people on our hands.

"We'd tell them about the exchange program," he said, "and they'd assume we were lying, since they'd had so many problems with previous managers. It was difficult to establish credibility. Some people probably thought we'd discovered oil under their lot, or something similar."

One of their primary concerns involved lot owners in Rotonda Heights, Rotonda Lakes and Rotonda Villas. "Their lots were not improved when we arrived in 1986," Futterer said. "Getting those three subdivisions' infrastructure complete was a mammoth task, one that didn't have high visibility but was of critical importance."

Another action Penzell took quickly in 1986 was to make Rotonda West Utility Corporation a separate, independent entity, where before it had operated as a component part of Cape Cave Corporation.

In time, Penzell had Rotonda Properties, Inc. functioning on a day to day basis through operating companies—Rotonda West Utilities Corporation, Rotonda Construction Corporation, Rotonda Golf & Country Club Corporation, Rotonda Corporation and Penn Properties Group, Inc. the management entities for Rotonda Properties and its subsidiaries.

"When Penzell's group came in they did a lot of good things," said Pat Stottsberry. "The other groups took more out than they put in."

A longtime Rotonda women's golf champion, Stottsberry was understandably pleased that under Penzell, golf course development became visibly active.

In October 1986, Oakland Hills formally became the Rotonda Golf & Country Club. In December came the shock of the increase of the initiation fee to three thousand dollars.

Futterer spoke the language of a marketer, saying, "Rotonda's golf product is one of Florida's most exciting." A membership campaign was started, "so that we can turn our focus to expanding the golf product."

In January 1987, excitement began to build as word spread that new golf courses were, in fact, in prospect. When plans were formally announced for golf in Pebble Beach and Windward it was almost anti-climatic. The news was met initially with skepticism by many who felt they had been burned enough by developer promises. But it seemed real enough.

To begin with, Penzell brought in Sam Maraffi as head golf pro, succeeding personable young Bob Ridge, who moved over to Lemon Bay Golf Club. Maraffi had been head pro at Raintree, where Penzell had been restructuring, and would now manage Rotonda's golf operations. Maraffi had started as a caddy in Pittsburgh, then spent thirteen years at Raintree. He was a Class A-1 PGA member.

Then, in September 1987, after a summer filled with flying rumors— one of the Rotonda community's favorite and often destructive pastimes—the *Sarasota Herald-Tribune* carried a column by golf writer Dave Laubach, headed: "Rotonda West May Yet Get More Courses."

"Sam Maraffi hopes to generate new excitement at Rotonda this year," Laubach wrote. "But the 3,500 residents of Rotonda West . . . want more than excitement, they want golf courses."

Laubach's article came close to resurrecting part of *The Vision*. He wrote that James Penzell had disclosed to him a plan that would have seven golf courses open for play within sixteen years. Penzell himself later confirmed that this was part of his long-range plan.

At the time Laubach's column came out construction was again booming at Rotonda. Twelve homes were being built each month. The ITA (Improvement Trust Account) then contained $22 million. According to Laubach, the cost to build each new course exceeded $1 million, and the existing course (Oakland Hills) had been appraised at $1.4 million in 1986.

Meanwhile, golf course architect John LaFoy was "letting nature run its course," in his planning of the Windward course on eighty acres, of which thirty-five were water. At the same time, Penzell had retained D. J. DeVictor, of golf course architects DeVictor & Langham, Atlanta. DeVictor was designing and laying out Rotonda's Pebble Beach, with considerable assistance from the late James Vann.

Vann was manager of property services for the developer, and was a man much admired by Rotondans who knew him. A North Carolinian, Vann "loved everything that was green or wet," said Bob Antes. "He loved the outdoors and went to great lengths to bring beauty to his work, of which he was justly proud. He deserves much of the credit for whatever is beautiful around The Hills golf course."

Vann died tragically in a 1992 auto accident at the junction of Boundary Boulevard and Rebel Court, where a four-way stop was subsequently installed. Just prior to his death, Vann had revised the sand traps on The Hills golf course.

By 1989, Futterer was talking enthusiastically about new courses as a boon to his marketing effort. He noted that the existing club then had four hundred members, "about the correct number for a club with eighteen holes of golf," he said.

He related the building of the Windward course to home development in that subdivision, pointing out that strong marketing would bring more residents to Rotonda, and this would support more golf facilities.

"John LaFoy has given us an executive course with character and devilment," Futterer said, a statement most area golfers would accept.

Windward opened for play in 1989, followed by Pebble Beach in 1990. Windward was later renamed The Cape Haze Links. Pebble Beach was also renamed The Palms, in deference to the more famous course on the Monterey Peninsula, whose owners formally requested that Rotonda not encroach on their worldwide reputation.

"We initially tried The Beaches," Futterer said, "but they still complained, so we planted more palm trees and called it The Palms."

With three golf courses now operating, initiation fees had also risen again, to five thousan1d dollars.

While they loved having three courses, many residents now began to express concern that the club was becoming a place for the affluent, although it was still conceded to be "the best golf bargain anywhere."

New York Police Department retiree John Lawson summed up the reaction of many, saying "In the old days you weren't compelled to spend forty dollars, which many now resent." Lawson had been president of the Men's Golf Association in 1978. He was referring to the new clubhouse "monthly minimum."

"These days they cater to a younger, more affluent crowd," Lawson noted, ruefully. "The older people just can't keep up. Look at all the FOR SALE signs in Oakland Hills."

While they enjoyed the new Palms golf course, many felt its clubhouse was built by "someone who didn't understand basic architecture, far less golf," to quote one golfer.

"It's got a perfect location, "he pointed out, "elevated on a hill where it could have had a panoramic view of the course. So, what do they do? They close it in. It's claustrophobic inside, and the view is blocked on all sides. Stupid. And that mop art on the wall . . . " the speaker just shook his head.

Even the new courses come in for mild criticism, many golfers arguing that The Hills, designed by Jim Petrides, who was not a golf architect, is "a better track than The Palms."

Pat Stottsberry had some observations. With the credibility of her former club championship titles, Stottsberry could also speak as state representative for Sarasota, Manatee and Charlotte counties of the Florida State Women's Golf Association.

Paul and Pat Stottsberry had moved to Rotonda in 1978, from Illinois, and loved it. "There was no initiation fee for golf then, and we could use our own golf cart," she said. "It didn't even bother us when the developer was in Chapter 11. We had our golf course, the sewers were in, and there wasn't much more we needed.

"The Hills is pretty tough for women," Stottsberry said. "The back nine is long and hard to par."

Stottsberry said that a woman with a twelve handicap will drive 150 yards, and hit her second shot 120 yards, a total of 270 yards. She points out that the par fours on the back nine [holes] are mostly over 300 yards for women. "Tough," she says. "Personally, I'd put the women's tee on nine back where it used to be. Otherwise the front nine is pretty good."

Stottsberry rates The Palms a good course for women, but would like longer par fives, and would move the ninth tee back and to the right, "away from that tree that blocks part of the fairway for us."

Another former champion, Helen Waldron, said, "They made a mistake when they built The Links. Too much water to go over. It's not for retired people unless they're good golfers. You lose balls like crazy and just get frustrated."

The men criticize mainly number six and number sixteen at The Palms. Said one, "Number six would be a super hole if the green was back another fifty yards. That was the plan, but they let some homeowner talk them into shortening it to preserve his privacy. On number sixteen, the gold tee should be moved fifteen yards forward and fifteen yards right."

However, golfing Rotondans were pleased with Penzell's development of the additional golf courses, and most are satisfied with their varied characters.

Penzell was also credited with investing over $30 million in new infrastructure, making a serious effort to beautify the community, initiating an aggressive building program with qualified independent builders, and cooperating in getting the L. A. Ainger and Vineland schools completed.

He was also applauded for addressing the long-term needs of the community for potable water and a good sewer system. It was Penzell's regime that finally got the Crom water tank in the hub connected into that system.

All in all, by 1990 there was general contentment at Rotonda.

I Wouldn't Live Anywhere Else

G ALEN CUSTARD, who joined Penzell's management team in 1986, conceded that events had conspired to divert Cavanagh's attention from startup of the reservoir they had built with such fanfare to support their R. O. water treatment plant.

Custard supervised the Rotonda West Utility Corporation, which was operated day-to-day by Rotonda resident Hugh Sumrall. The reservoir was finally connected in 1989.

"We're lucky they built the tank," Custard said, "even if they never put it in service. Before that we had about one fourth of a day's water supply. If we'd had a significant fire, we'd have had to let it burn."

As with the randomness of their lot sales, prior developers mismanaged the water operation, Custard charged. "Nobody took time to figure Rotonda's needs for potable water, or for fire-flow protection through the seven hundred-fifty community fire hydrants," he said.

When Penzell's group came in, they immediately focused on water service. "We quickly had eighteen people working, mostly in the field. The plants operated twenty-four hours a day, and we made this into a service operation that we constantly improve," said Custard.

Custard also made two interesting points that related to running the Rotonda utility. He emphasized Penzell's efforts to establish cooperative relationships with government agencies, rather than to continue the confrontational approach of prior developers.

Today, he said, while the county regulates water rates, the Department of Environmental Regulation (DER) is involved "on a daily basis, and is the single biggest source of the increased cost of bringing you water.

"Costs to bring water out of the ground haven't changed much, but the cost of obtaining all the necessary permits, and the bureaucratic entanglements you go through, make it expensive," Custard said.

He also mentioned the Coral Creek dam, which some residents refer to as "that infamous dam," because they hold it responsible for Rotonda's lack of Gulf access for their boats.

The dam, at the northeast corner of Windward, was put in originally by the Vanderbilt brothers to keep the salt water side of Coral Creek from intruding further north.

"I don't know why they did that," Custard said, "but it would have been more difficult to find fresh water around here without it. We own that dam now. It's not an operable structure, but it has a controlled outfall," meaning, apparently, that the dam can be opened if excessive rainfall threatens canal flooding.

Like the water system, the sewer system was in dire need of attention when Penzell's group took over in 1986.

"There was an old metal tank that was rusting away," Custard said. "It should have been abandoned. And they had a sewage treatment facility turning out spray irrigation for open fields and golf areas. We'd be shut down if we used that approach today.

"Essentially we had to modernize the whole process, build new aeration tanks because the old ones were, in a word, disgusting," said Custard. "We had to rebuild the clarifier, which was barely functioning."

As a result of Penzell's modernization, residents who were used to a puny fifty PSI (pounds per square inch) of water pressure when they took a shower now get about seventy-two PSI.

Custard expressed pride in what his group had achieved with the utility, based on how they found it coming in. "When I first came here," he said, "I'd catch little bass and throw them into the holding pond. If I'm here another three or four years, I know I'll catch a ten pounder from that pond."

He won't. Custard isn't here today. But Rotonda fishing enthusiasts, like Neal Cennamo, might like to test his theory.

Another Penzell team member was Robert Underwood who had also worked with him in Charlotte, North Carolina. In 1990 Underwood came in to manage Cape Cave Corporation and became president of the Waterway Maintenance Association.

In April of that year Underwood informed POA President John Meadows that it was time to turn over the WMA to POA responsibility.

"We felt the shape of the canals was not such that we wanted to take it over," Meadows said, "however, we didn't have a lot of choice. We chose not to get into costly litigation."

Underwood wrote, "Your association now owns 456 acres of common property and canals in Rotonda West and is responsible . . . for these assets."

An amended constitution and new bylaws for the new association were agreed upon. The proposed budget for 1991 called for assessment income, at sixty dollars per lot, of $489,000. Of this, $250,000 would go directly into maintenance. The balance would support administration, certain community programs—including $5,000 for "fish stocking"—and operating and other reserves.

The infamous Waterway Maintenance Association had now evolved into the Rotonda West Association (RWA).

That was fine for Rotonda West, but what about the rest of Rotonda—outside the circle?

Outside the circle, it turned out, nobody was handling the associations, to the extent that any associations existed at all.

Enter Anne Underwood, wife of Robert Underwood. She grabbed the bull by the horns, formed Gulf Coast Management, and proceeded to do for the subdivisions outside the circle what the RWA had done in Rotonda West, essentially maintain all lakes, ponds, and public greenbelts.

In short order, Underwood was managing Rotonda Lakes for 3,038 property owners, Sands North for 2,400, Cape Haze/Windward for some 1,600, the forty patio homes in Windward and Riverhouse condominiums.

There were instant problems, of course.

In Underwood's first meeting with her Windward constituents, forty-two of whom showed up, "All I remember is that they were outraged that the sign at the entrance said Rotonda," Underwood said. "They didn't want to be associated with it." She commented that, even in the early 1990s, a degree of polarization still existed between Rotonda and Cape Haze.

Underwood also received threats. Not surprising, she suggested, since for years Rotonda lot owners heard nothing but silence on area maintenance, then, out of the blue, they get a bill from a company they had never heard of.

The threat Underwood most remembers came from a telephone caller in the Miami area who identified herself, said she owned property in Rotonda Sands, had received a bill for maintenance around her lot and was angry. Somewhat incoherently she said she had a gun and would not hesitate to make the trip to Rotonda to kill those responsible for harassing her.

"I laughed at first," Anne Underwood said, "Then I played the tape again and called the sheriff. I mean, Miami isn't that far away.

"Actually, it was an absolute nightmare," she said of her start-up. "Here we were contacting people virtually around the world who owned lots. They were irate, understandably so."

For example, while maintenance organizations had been established in The Lakes and Sands North in 1972, neither residents nor lot owners seemed aware that they were mandatory members. Now, all of a sudden, they found that they were being assessed . . . sixty dollars for The Lakes, later reduced to forty, and forty-two dollars and fifty cents for Sands North.

Why was nothing done earlier? Underwood doesn't know.

"All I know is we tried to get things organized on a sensible, paying and effective basis," she said. "It took us several months just to get the proper names and addresses from county property deeds and plat records."

However, like the POA and the RWA within the circle, Underwood brought order to lake, pond and greenbelt maintenance in the rest of Rotonda. More credit to Penzell's management.

Meanwhile, even the POA seemed satisfied with the new Rotonda management. By April 1988 it was declaring "a cooperative association . . . and believe we are negotiating with people of integrity." That, in itself, would be a first in Rotonda's history.

In 1989, still euphoric, the POA told its members that the developer "has continued to impress the skeptics with their program to improve Rotonda."

Even with regard to the original vision, Bill Futterer said, " . . . it hasn't changed a whole lot. We've just adjusted its progress in terms of timing."

Attorney Guy Batsel, associated with Rotonda from its beginning, said, "There was a major swing in credibility and marketability of Rotonda in 1988 or 1989. I think it has a very positive image now."

Batsel credits Penzell for the change. "Instead of just defending lawsuits and retaining lawyers, Jim Penzell did positive things. After all, a great deal of money was sitting in Tallahassee accruing interest. Finally somebody came along with enough credibility to convince the regulators that it should be released to advance the purpose for which it was in escrow. This was very positive."

By the early 1990s, according to Futterer, the sales focus was to establish a $50,000 to $80,000 home market at Rotonda, making it a major retiree market for the 1990s. One problem he anticipated was the county impact fee which was imposed on all new construction. At almost $2000 per unit, he felt that the cost increase caused by the fee might be a problem, especially when imposed on modest housing .

Another continuing minor irritant: the telephone system being identified as Cape Haze, the post office as Placida (They still declined to change all their directories to accommodate a local change.) and the zip code dividing in the middle of Rotonda.

"These are political matters outside the scope of Rotonda management," Futterer said.

As this narrative concludes, in 1994, the Rotonda community is of age. Three golf courses are operating. Home building is active, with many builders busy moving west to east through Rotonda. Roads, water and sewers are being completed in The Villas and The Heights. New residents live in The Lakes, near the new Elks building.

Don Pedro Island is still a jewel, still open for the residents' enjoyment. It's a state park now, but the buildings have been refurbished, showers, toilets, and fresh water are available, and private entrepreneurs offer the scenic voyage across the Intracoastal to Don Pedro's mile of pristine beach. Almost as *The Vision* promised, before *Reality* set in.

As of March 31, 1994, Penzell's contract expired and Simanco V, Inc. became managers of Rotonda Properties for Citicorp on an interim basis, pending the outright sale of Rotonda in its entirety to another owner.

Penzell and his team departed, but he expressed interest in participating in the bidding and remaining in Rotonda's future, so is one likely bidder.

Before he left Penzell had said, "We have tried to fulfill the obligations we inherited. If we're successful in our acquisition effort, then we look forward to the opportunity to finish what we started.

"It was fortuitous that the basic land assemblage concept of Rotonda was carried out in Florida. It couldn't happen today anywhere else. It couldn't even be done in Florida."

The question still is Rotonda's future. Who will the new developer be? Who will manage the golf operations? The Rotonda West Association is firmly established inside the circle, but the outside subdivisions are just beginning to face the realities of roadway, canal and greenbelt maintenance where the county has not yet accepted maintenance responsibilities. Change is sometimes disturbing, but inevitable.

In time, there could be myriad associations helping the community to function—the RWA inside the circle and as many as ten other associations representing the outside subdivisions' property owners where membership is mandatory. Then there's the POA, with membership open to all. That's the extent of the community's political and operating structure. Rotonda is still an unincorporated district within mostly-unincorporated Charlotte County.

As for the residents, most wouldn't live anywhere else.

"To this day we have the greatest bunch of people here," said Mimi Edelstein. "We enjoy each other and we're concerned about each other. It's that kind of community."

Said Ed Hennessey, "I love it. I know I couldn't survive back home [Geneva, New York] any more."

"It's a wonderful place," said Joe Tringali, one of the movers and shakers who made it so. "I wouldn't live anywhere else."

"Best golf value anywhere," said Allyn Taylor, a 1990 arrival. Taylor speaks for a group of about twenty resident and non-resident golfers, mostly recent arrivals.

"An excellent long-term investment for us," said Harry Virtue.

George Manyak said, "This is the best deal in the world, and I think most people here agree with that."

Says Ed Melton, "We've had a ball here. Wouldn't live anywhere else."

"We're sitting on our porch," said Jerry Ullrich, "a nice breeze is blowing, the thermometer reads ninety-four. Dorothy said, 'Is this the worst it's going to get?' I said, 'Yes.' So we sold out in Baltimore and made it final here."

John Meadows: "It's been a lot of fun . . . a sense of accomplishment."

"A great place to live," said Jack Labar.

Rotonda even enjoys its own weather phenomenon. "I don't know how it works," one resident said. "We can have storms all around but when the front gets here it seems to split. Part goes up the coast and part goes up the Myakka [River] leaving us with sunshine. It's a special place."

So, launched in 1969, Rotonda has grown, despite setbacks, to a community of almost 2,800 homes and more than 6,000 residents by the summer of 1994. Today, from the original 35,000 platted lots, there are still almost 22,000 buildable, with 5,715 still unsold. Major development is complete, meaning roads, water and sewer lines are in place.

On land with a fascinating history, Rotonda grew on unfulfilled promises of a *Vision*. The *Vision* succumbed to *Reality*.

But the *Reality* of Rotonda is wonderful!

Epilogue

THE PLAN WAS to conclude this history here, at the end of Rotonda's 25th year. But as I switched off the computer, two events took place that may signal that Rotonda's second quarter-century may be as exciting and uncertain as its first.

In early September, 1994, Simanco V, Inc., the interim manager of Rotonda, announced the sale of the development by Citicorp to the 41/75 Corporation, an investment group named after highways near the property. The sale encompasses all the unsold properties, The Rotonda West Utility Company and the golf operations.

The 41/75 Corporation includes Pittsburgh investor Richard K. Means, Jr., Powell River Ventures of New England, Florida realtor John Zielenbach and Gary Littlestar, who is known around Rotonda from his former association with James Penzell.

Community reaction seemed favorable. Comments in the clubhouse focused on the new group's experience with real estate development and its successful transformation of another real estate purchase in 1993, Tampa Palms, into a desirable golf community in Hillsborough County.

Golfers in particular were excited about reports that if the 41/75 group closed the deal, professional golfer Raymond Floyd might buy the golf operations. "Floyd wouldn't put his name to anything but the best in golf," was a common view. Even more positive were reliable reports in late September that the funds to build additional golf courses were securely held in an investment trust account, making the next course likely by 1997 if Rotonda's home-building pace holds up.

There were of course, the usual questions: Who are these people? . . . What on earth is 41/75? . . . What are their plans for our community?. . . Will it all cost me more?

On September 16, the *St. Petersburg Times* quoted a 41/75 spokesperson saying the corporation planned to close on the Rotonda purchase by the end of the year.

Also on September 16, a class-action lawsuit was filed in Dade County Circuit Court in Miami by Louis Robles of the law firm Robles & Gonzales against Citicorp and its subsidiary, Rotonda Holdings, Inc., the Cape Cave and Cape Haze Corporations and several prominent accounting firms including Price Waterhouse, Ernst & Young, Arthur Andersen & Company and KPMG Peat Marwick. All were firms associated with Rotonda in the past.

The charges—in what seems to be deja vu—are reminiscent of the early 1980s Binstein saga. The lawsuit alleges, among other things, that the defendants failed to make development improvements promised to Rotonda property buyers; failed to transfer road responsibility to the county, and failed to complete promised development on time. The accounting defendants are included because they failed to disclose "significant liabilities" that they knew would adversely affect Rotonda's development.

Robles is demanding a jury trial, seeking compensatory damages for the plaintiffs, recision of all contracts, and payment of all litigation costs, including attorneys' fees. He also notes in his complaint that "Robles & Gonzalez has the financial and legal resources to meet the substantial costs . . . associated with this litigation." This is taken to mean that plaintiffs need to put up no money for the lawsuit.

Robles, who filed the suit on behalf of one Janet Eick "and all others similarly situated," wrote a letter to Rotonda property owners soliciting their support for the suit. Rotonda residents are now waiting for the other shoe to drop. The majority appear thoroughly happy with Rotonda. Many recall that the buy-in to Binstein's project was $475 per lot and reportedly no one recovered anything through the project.

Robles was quoted in a September 17 article, written by Tom Matrullo of the *Sarasota Herald-Tribune*, as indicating that the number of plaintiffs could eventually reach 20,000. In his complaint, Robles states his belief that "over 70,000 individual citizens" have bought Rotonda property, signing contracts to do so.

On learning of the lawsuit, residents were concerned that it might jeopardize the pending sale of the property to 41/75. They decided to demonstrate their support of the sale and hopefully deter other property owners from joining Eick in the class-action suit. They have held community meetings, circulated a petition and sought other ways to alert distant property owners to the potential danger that this unwanted litigation could lower their property value. Several hundred have signed their names to an ad opposing the lawsuit in the *Englewood Sun-Herald*.

It seems that the community is at work again. As Rotonda resident Frank Clancy said, "We who live here should band together and show support for our community."

And so, Rotonda moves ahead into its second quarter-century, a land-based schooner sailing towards an unknown horizon. On land with a fascinating past, full of folklore and fact, the community has grown to a delightful *Reality*, despite unfilfilled promises of a *Vision* and an uncertain but potentially exciting future.

Rotonda Timeline

1885   First sale of Rotonda land . . . to railroad

1951   Vanderbilt brothers purchase Rotonda land

1969   Cavanagh Leasing Corp. acquires Rotonda land
First public offering of Rotonda West
First filing of Rotonda deed restrictions

1970   Surveyor stakes center of Rotonda West circle
Rotonda West grand opening

1971   Reverse osmosis water treatment plant built
Cavanagh claims more than 15,000 Rotonda lots sold
Kaars move in, become first family in residence
Sunday golf course (Hills) opens for play

1972   Rotonda post office sub-station opens
Women's Golf Association elects Helen Waldron president
Crom reservoir water tank built
Fiesta Association formed by Mike Saunders

1973   Community Church organizational meeting held
Sports/recreational complex completed in The Shores
"The Superstars" first events
Riverhouse condominium complex completed
Rotonda West Lions Club formed
U.S. Coast Guard Auxiliary chartered
Clubhouse was scheduled to be completed
Rotonda West Woman's Club established
First Faith Church service in Community Center

1974   POA elects Joseph A. Tringali first president
        Western Apartments open on Boundary Boulevard

1975   Cavanagh files for Chapter 11 bankruptcy protection
        Curbside mail delivery begins in Rotonda West
        Cape Cave names Jim Petrides on-site manager
        FTC adds Rotonda to its land use investigation

1976   Deltona assumes management of Rotonda
        Cavanagh emerges from Chapter11 bankruptcy

1977   Richard Bean elected president of POA
        Joe Tringali becomes County Commissioner
        Deltona announces new Waterway Maintenance Association
        James Graham elected president of POA

1978   POA files lawsuit against Cavanagh
        Cavanagh's casino investments become public

1979   Richard Tanner elected POA president
        Class-action lawsuit filed against Cavanagh
        Land Resources Corp. assumes Rotonda management
        Jury finds for Cavanagh in lawsuit verdict

1980   Major bridge construction program begins
        Rotonda Properties group acquires Rotonda

1981   Binstein arrives, charges Cavanagh with fraud
        Public hearings on 400 percent utility rate increase

1983   Francis Labar elected president of POA
        Antes Agreement issued from circuit court

1984   Revised deed restrictions issued by county court
        State acquires Don Pedro Island for more than $6 million

1986   James Penzell assumes Rotonda management
        Oakland Hills becomes Rotonda Golf & Country Club
        Ed Hennessey elected president of POA

1988   Joe Obey elected POA president

1989 Cape Haze golf course (Links) opens in Windward
1990 John Meadows elected POA president
Pebble Beach course, later renamed Palms, opens
Property owners receive first maintenance bills
Rotonda West Association (RWA) activated

1991 Ullrich elected president of POA
Ullrich steps down, Carvalho becomes POA president
Ullrich elected first RWA president
Carvalho resigns, Bill Coy becomes POA president

1992 Fred Warner elected second RWA president

1994 Earle Simpson elected POA president
Simanco V, Inc. assumes interim management
Rotonda reported sold to 41/45 investment group
Class-action lawsuit filed against Citicorp

Endnotes

[1] Great Outdoors Publishing Co., St. Petersburg, Florida.; 1959

[2] Published by Pineapple Press; Englewood, Florida; 1984

[3] "The Superstars" is a registered trademark of Candid Productions, Inc.

[4] Referred to in text hereafter as POA, rather than RWPOA.

About the Author

Jack Alexander was born in Edinburgh, Scotland in January, 1926 and served in the Royal Marine Commandos during World War II. After the war, he studied journalism and political economy at Edinburgh University.

In 1948, Alexander emigrated to the United States, where he became a reporter for the *Cincinnati Post*, then was a news correspondent for six business newspapers published by Fairchild Publications. In 1958 he joined Formica Corporation and rose to director of public relations and advertising. In 1978 he left corporate life to become a free-lance business and marketing writer in New York.

Alexander moved to Rotonda in 1990 where he continues to write, and play golf and bridge.